# *AMBASSADOR ATMANIRBHAR BHARAT*

ATTORNEY
MANISH N. JADHAV

BlueRose ONE.com
Stories Matter
New Delhi • London

**BLUEROSE PUBLISHERS**
India | U.K.



For permissions requests or inquiries regarding this publication, please contact:

BLUEROSE PUBLISHERS
www.BlueRoseONE.com
info@bluerosepublishers.com
+91 8882 898 898
+44 07342408967

ISBN: 978-93-5989-713-4

Cover Design: Sadhna Kumari
Typesetting: Pooja Sharma

First Edition: May 2024

*In the Memory of my beloved Late father,*

*Shri. Nanasaheb Jadhav (Rao)*

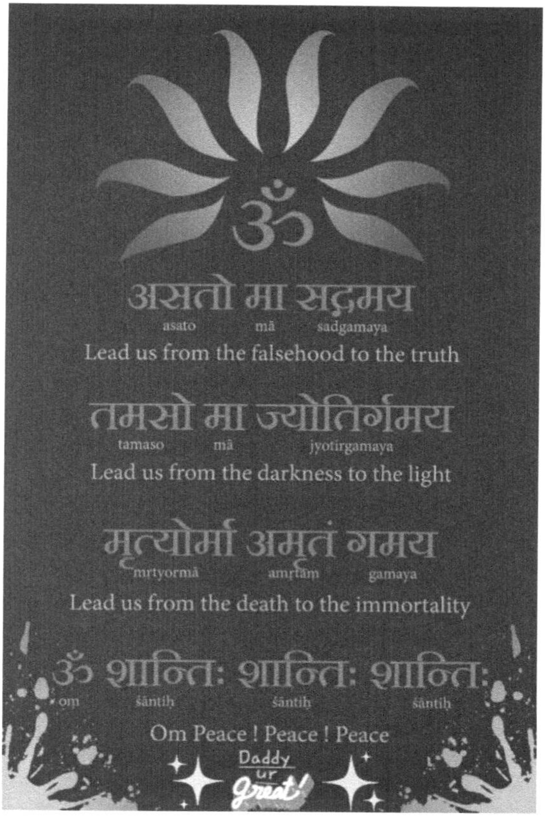


*PITRU-DEVA-BHAVA*

*(Dear Daddy, my dawn even today begins with you, and my day ends with beautiful memories which we together cherished! I Love You)*

# Preface

**"Take up one idea. Make that one idea your life – think of it, dream of it, live on that idea. Let the brain, muscle, nerves, every part of your body, be full of that idea, and just leave every other idea alone." Swami Vivekananda.**

I decided to write this book because, I took up an idea of 'Atmanirbhar Bharat'. I wanted to share what I have learned through failures, vis-a-vis gained from success. I also wanted to provide all 'Bhartiyas' a short history on Atmanirbhar Bharat and how can we all become self-reliant/resilient without losing our oneness. This is my story, how I became Atmanirbhar.

This is neither an autobiography nor a self-help book, because the reader read with their own perspective and experience. Therefore, I leave this to the readers to decide what this book is for them. But, one thing I am sure, that when the readers complete reading this book, he or she will understand why it is important to become self-reliant (Atmanirbhar)?

The reason why, I am so much inclined to the vision of 'Atmanirbhar Bharat' is because, in today's era of cyber security, artificial intelligence and sustainable development goals, pandemic management etc, have become essential part of our life. It is also crucial to study the conflicts in between Russia and Ukraine, juxtapose Israel and Palestine. Arab and Iran conflicts included.

These lessons are important due to the reason, that, if Bharat does not become Atmanirbhar? In coming years, who's going to gain are China & Pakistan? Whole world has come to know about their motives and intentions. Therefore, the one and only solution to this problem is to make our Bharat Atmanirbhar in all possible ways; because, we shall not forget that; "Strength respects Strength" as far as national security and integrity is concerned.

In coming years, whole world will be facing serious challenges, such as; climate change, terrorism, corruption, conflicts, wars, etc. which will result into instability in national and international markets, posing a direct threat to economies of small and big countries alike.

Therefore, the countries which are prepared, the nations which are Atmanirbhar will survive and will not loose their states stability and vitality.

In order to keep our nation stable, it is the duty of every Indian to start working on fundamental duties enshrined in our constitution. Eventually, transferring that reliance & resilience from self to society.

# Forward

One fine day I was busy doing my gardening work, suddenly Manish came to me and said, 'I want to do something more creative, contributive, and crucial for our country'. I replied, that you are already giving your spare time to various social activities, environmental promotions, and human rights protection. Moreover, you are always ready to help the ones who really need your help and guidance, by going an extra mile! What more do you want to do for the nation now? He said, I want to write a book! For a minute, I just stared at him, because I myself was puzzled, as he did not have any experience in writing a book. No doubt! He has authored many articles, also written many plaints and drafted many Writs, PILs, and contracts, but definitely, writing a book is altogether a different thing. So, I, asked him - On what topic do you want to write a book? He immediately replied, that he wanted to write a book on "Atmanirbhar Bharat". Moreover, he added by saying 'People & Google', both have made me 'Ambassador of Atmanirbhar Bharat', therefore I seriously want to write a book on the same and even share my own journey of Atmanirbharta vis-à-vis shaksharta and also serve and contribute, my time and energy for creating --- A Bharat which will be Atmanirbhar in all its ways and possible forms! I went into my little library, came back immediately, & handed him a blank notebook and said --- 'Your Journey Starts Here!

To conclude, firstly I will introduce myself; I am Sonali, currently pursuing my PhD from, SPPU-IITM jointly in the subject of environmental sciences. I have been actively involved in public policy making, mostly in the field of, climate change, ecology, & water management, since last couple of decades, and was recognized and rewarded as UN-SDG-Talent (United Nations Sustainable Development Group). As a researcher, writer and an eco-agro-Prenuer, I was lucky to travel to various parts of our country (many times even other countries), during which I found and observed that, there so many things which, we as a union of Bharat needs to prove and improve, in order to truly become Atmanirbhar! I am glad to say that, I have co-authored this book by sharing vital and incomparable thing's about my husband i.e. attorney Manish Jadhav, more particularly in the three chapters in part-II of this book. I am his wife who is not only his partner for life, but also his friend, a team mate, a volunteer in his social organisation, and work, and importantly a mirror who shows him his error, in order to make him free from the error.

Secondly, I would say that, this book is neither a perfect piece of papers nor is it trying to claim something, but it is definitely a road map for future of Bharat – which brightly appears to me as 'Atmanirbhar and Viksit'.

Third thing, to be very frank, we together as citizen of this country, have a moral responsibility to create naya Bharat, which will be full of compassion and passion. But for making our nation great as it was in ancient times, we all need to work hard and find smart solutions to the current problems of unemployment, poverty, population & pollution etc. Let's unite to make our motherland future proof from all kinds of adversaries by making it Atmanirbhar.

Last but never the least, I would firmly say that, Manish is the right person to write this book, because he himself, is a living example of being an "all round Ambassador of Atmanirbhar Bharat" throughout his life. People often, see his success, but let me tell you, I have seen him struggling, I have seen him sacrificing so many things and I have seen him serving the needy, because SUCCESS, is not one day job! He has already took a pledge or Sankalp, towards making this country of ours self-reliant, self-resilient and self-sufficient.

I wish him and all the readers of our motherland --- Bharat! All the very best for being committed to fulfil the dream of Atmanirbhar & Viksit Bharat, shown to us by *Hon'ble Prime Minister Shri. Narendra Modi ji.*

**Smt. Sonali M. Jadhav**

**Co-author (AAB)**

# Acknowledgements

Ambassador of Atmanirbhar Bharat is not only about me or my story, it's about Bharat.

It's about the countless countrymen or Bhartiya's like me who are intending and trying to make our country Atmanirbhar in all its sectors by changing ourselves first and eventually setting a pattern of Self-Reliant mind-set in every individual.

I would like to thank;

**Firstly**, my family and friends, without their support I am incomplete!

**Secondly**, my Gurus and Mentors whom I always remember every day in my prayers!

**Thirdly**, MyGov, UNITAR, Google, Jio, because of them, it was easy for me to earn certificates and insights success, Fox Story and at least a dozen of magazine's along with the publisher of this book i.e. **Blue Rose Publishers**, who told my story to the world!

**Most importantly**, Shri. Narendra Modi ji and his team of Atmanirbhars for their commitment to build a super Bharat and numerous people who pray for me and wellbeing of Bharat!

**Last but not the least**, all Bhartiya's who are starving and eager to make Bharat Atmanirbhar!

# Contents

# PART - I

## Chapter – 1

# Who Coined the Term Atmanirbhar Bharat?

**"The difference between what we do and what we are capable of doing would suffice to solve most of the world's problems" – Attorney M. K. Gandhi (Mahatma Gandhi)**

**Introduction:**

It was in the year 1919, month of October, also the birth month of Mahatma Gandhi. Gandhiji while delivering a speech at 'Bhagini Samaj', Mumbai, he stressed the need for making India - Atmanirbhar.

The exact words used by the Mahatma in his hindi speech were;

"Hindustan ko Atmanirbhar Bharat hona sikhna hi hoga" (India must learn to be self-reliant).

The speech which he gave in hindi was in context of the benefits of the 'Charkha' or spinning wheel which could be a source of income for women.

He further said, "There is no other occupation in which millions of women can engage while staying at home. It does not call for much intelligence. India must learn to be self-reliant.

While saying this, Gandhiji mostly focused on three W's – (a) Women, (b) Work, (c) Wages.

Recently during the Covid-19 pandemic most of us were locked in our own houses and premises thought of 'Working from Home', but I think, so the real (WFH) began during 1919.

Today we talk about gender equality, but Gandhiji's vision was to make every Indian, most importantly the women to be financially independent by earning to satisfy the means of herself and her family.

Accordingly, wages drawn by the women would add to the male or family income resulting into surplus and savings of the family and society.

Moreover, in the same speech, he also stated that "gender equality"

"When India produces brave men and women, we shall become self-reliant", and if the nation could show that bravery, "we shall be free right away".

Mahatma Gandhi, himself was attorney at law in South Africa. During his stay in South Africa, he used to provide justice and also fought for dignity of the Indians living in South Africa.

But he lived on one principle 'Simple Living and Higher Thinking'. He had put more emphasis on things like; tolerance, non-violence, decentralization of powers which, according to him, were essential for the people and welfare of the society.

Gandhiji was known as 'Mahatma' – because of various things or sacrifices he made in his life. Mahatma is a combination of two words 'Mahan' + 'Atma', which means a person having an evolved / great soul.

The reason why he used to say that – "My life is my message", because firstly, he lived his life on very limited means, secondly, he was very disciplined man and valued time, thirdly, he liked his surrounding clean and tidy, he used to do most of his works by himself – which he called was his 'Swadharma'.

Nevertheless, he always asked the Indian people to inculcate the idea of 'Swadeshi' in their mind set by propagating – "Be Indian and buy Indian", With intention to recreate a self-reliant society.

Notably; even today Indian markets are flooded by Chinese goods? Can't we inculcate the same idea of 'Swadeshi' and only buy 'Make in India' goods? If we decide not to purchase Chinese goods, we can hit them with power of wallets without using our bullets (For example, Galvan was an eye-opening incident where they wanted to forcefully grab a piece of land without letting us know however, the brave Indian soldiers gave them a befitting reply, but precious lives were lost; therefore, if we reduce dependency on their cheap quality goods, we can avoid our own money to hit us back by them.

**Former Leaders who promoted the Idea of Self-Reliant Nation:**

Eventually, **Prime Minister Indira Gandhi**, in her address to the 'National Development Council' in the year 1976, used phrase self-reliance a number of times, she emphasizes on making India Atmanirbhar. Late Prime Minister, Smt. Indira Gandhi in an address to the National Development Council was very much concerned about our country's weaknesses and therefore she, used the phrase "A Nation's strength ultimately consists in what it can be on its own, and not in what it can borrow from others" - putting here more emphasis on making India self-reliant in food, energy including finance Atmanirbharta.

**Dr. B. R. Ambedkar** use to say; 'Parliamentary democracy was meaningless unless it was geared to achieving the real goal of economic democracy', he meant - Financial Atmanirbharta.

**Shri. Atal Bihari Vajpayee**, was a staunch supporter of Atmanirbhar Bharat, nuclear test conducted in Pokhran, is an example that, he dared to conduct test, without fearing the sanctions imposed by western nations. During that period, many opposition leaders have severely criticized Atal ji, but aren't we Indian's proud today that we have our nuclear plant - This way self-reliant and resilient our country became in the field of deterrence.

**APJ. Abdul Kalam's Book** - India 2020 - is all about Atmanirbhar Bharat, as predicted by him much before, Covid-19 was all about making India self-reliant.

Atmanirbhar is reflected from Shivaji's 'Swarajya' to Gandhiji's 'Swadeshi' and Swami Vivekanandas 'Swadharma'.

**Atmanirbharta & Imprints:**

Later on, the baton of Atmanirbhar Bharat has been taken by our current Prime Minister and his team, by starting Atmanirbhar Bharat Abhiyan in 2020.

Leaders and policy makers who spoke on Atmanirbhar recently are as follows;

Defence Minister - **Rajnath Singh**

INS Imphal - Missile destroyed, Mumbai (Indian Navy) 75% indigenous content, enhanced stealth, features, State of Art equipment and weapons - a symbol of Atmanirbharta.

Recently, Union Home Minister, **Amit Shah** while addressing an event in Gandhinagar talked about the 'Aim to make 140 crore citizens of the country, including the poor, self-reliant (Atmanirbhar).

Gujrat Chief Minister: **Bhupendra Patel** added that poor people in our country have started living a self-reliant life as a result of Good Governance of 9 years by Union Government.

Finance Minister: **Smt. Nirmal Sitharaman,** said Atmanirbhar doesn't mean breaking ties with other Nations, on the contrary it does mean that building more stronger ties with the like-minded group's, companies, countries in the world.

**E.A.M: S. Jaishankar** himself is a living example and reflection of the term 'Atmanirbhar Bharat', and is always eager to promote Atmanirbhar Policies in our country.

**Shri. Nitin Gadkari,** is vital force behind the e-mobility, infrastructure and developing world class facilities and enhancing Atmanirbhar Bharat. He always says growth is not possible without capacity building and creating a reliant country. Atmanirbharta is seen and felt through his actions and orientations.

Economic Advisor: **Sanjeev Sanyal** – Atmanirbhar Bharat is about engaging with the rest of the World.

Ambassador. **Vikram Mistri** (who served as Indian Ambassador to China during crucial times of Covid-19), clearly said that; Atmanirbhar Bharat is a self-reliant India but definitely not a self-centric one.

Additionally , many foreign envoys and high office bearers have identified lot's of scope and potential in the concept of Atmanirbhar Bharat;

A) US Ambassador to India, **Kenneth Juster** in 2021, had said --- Atmanirbhar Bharat is an opportunity to increase business in India.

B) Netherland Ambassador to India, **Mr. Martin Van den Berg** was of the view that; Atmanirbhar Bharat is not only good news for India but also for the world.

C) France Ambassador said, Atmanirbhar Bharat will enhance defense partnership between both the countries on bilateral level. Which will create a gateway for make in India products in Europe via France.

D) Moreover, India has been optimistic to increase the supply chains across the globe, through Indian embassies, in many countries have already started Atmanirbhar campaigns, under its flagship of 'Make in India', wherein many products, produces, goods and even services are offered and promoted to optimum level, so that make in

India, products become a big brand worldwide.

E) Nevertheless, Atmanirbhar Bharat campaign and also schemes have not only enhanced the global image of our country, but it has resulted into export promotions of make in India & made in Bharat, goods world over --- from selling and supplying arms and ammunition to many countries under defense Atmanirbharta to producing iPhone and manufacturing various luxury brands in tie-ups with the international brands have become a reality in last three years.

**Conclusion**:

Atmanirbhar Bharat will be the new dawn of Asia, who will eventually replace the mainland, as a superpower and also will be super positioned, in coming decades. World will see Bharat, not only as self-reliant but more reliable friend as Vishwamitra and as mentor or tutor in form of Vishwa Guru in coming years.

Chapter – 2

# Why Our Prime Minister Invoked the Term 'Atmanirbhar Bharat' In 2020?

**'By Common endeavour we can raise the country to a new greatness, while a lack of unity will expose us to fresh calamities', SARDAR VALLABHAI PATEL**

## Atmanirbhar Bharat - Reel to Real insights:

As a whole world was facing huge turmoil due to the pandemic of Covid – 19, which tested the resilience of all nations. India under the leadership of Shri. Narendra Modi sought to convert the obstacles into opportunities.

We still remember the janta curfew which was followed by the 'LOCK DOWN', whereby a tiny virus showed the world that how can a virus, which cannot be seen through a naked eye, bring whole world to 'Standstill'.

India's response to the virus was immediate, as early actions by the government gave boost to our health care infrastructure thereby resulting in high recovery rates and successfully controlling the spread of Corona virus in the most populated country across the globe.

The International Monetary Fund, predicted that, the world economy may contract by over 3% (three percent) in the year 2020.

Therefore, it was thought to prepare India better for a new global economic order, the Union government under the leadership of Shri. Modi, identified five key pillars;

(1) Creating a new economy

(Prime Minister Mudra Yojana, boost to MSME's etc.)

(2) State of the art infrastructure

(Railways, airways, navigation, and roadways etc.

(3) Technology based delivery systems (Digi Locker)

(4) Leveraging India's youthful demography (Self & Society)

(5) Harnessing domestic demand ('Vocal for Local')

Along with the vaccination booster, a need was felt to boost our economy and therefore an economic stimulus package of US $270 billion, equivalent to 10% (ten percent) of India's GDP, under the new deal of 'Atmanirbhar Bharat Abhiyan was announced by the Union government.

In May 2020, our Prime Minister announced his "vision of Atmanirbhar Bharat" to shape the future of India, which aims to make our country self-reliant and resilient in all its forms, integrated with the global economy.

The idea of Atmanirbhar Bharat seeded its roots in India's longstanding commitment to sustainable development of all Bharat vasis and also for the global community, under our guiding principle of 'Vasudhaiva Kutumbakam', which literally means, 'whole world is one family'.

As our nation is home to 1/6$^{th}$ of humanity, success of our nation in achieving the global goals or SDG's will determine their outcome in the world. India is well aware of its responsibility and is committed to fully implement the 17 Goals defined under the United Nations Sustainable Development Goals (UNSDG), through various well-designed national schemes and programmes.

Whether it be the International Yoga Day or Swaach Bharat or NEP or Garib Kalyan or Women, Child and Youth Development, there are thousands of policies and effective implementation is also taking place nationally.

The policy is built on the fine formational pillars i.e. access, equity, quality, affordability and accountability – all of which are directly aligned to the SDG's.

It is vital to note that, the Indian Diaspora is known for its work ethic, discipline and contribution to the international community vis-à-vis Indian economy. This not only enriches our country but also plays a prominent role in making our future bright and successful.

Countries across the globe, show a growing interest in our nation and its potential to become an additional engine of growth; due to the simple reason that, we have the ability to provide a large pool of talented people and our governance mode is also enhanced by implementing more and more democratic reforms and rule of law, through the mixture of our democratic traditional and international standards.

*E.A.M: S. Jaishankar had said that;*

"The World may be on the threshold of a new decade; but India is poised to enter the next phase of its own evolution."

**Prime Minister/People/Policy - Forming a Growth Engine:**

Prior to Covid-19, Indians have faced tremendous problems during the demonetization and implementing the GST, but neither the Covid-19 nor for that matter demonetization / GST could stop our people in believing the central leadership, which came for change and successfully induced change in people, pattern and progress of our nation.

Today, a developing country like ours is sighted as an example - how it handled Covid-19 effectively? This was also the time when, Indian companies manufactured vaccines and exported them to various countries in the world. The effective leadership of Prime Minister is praised by many world Leaders, some of them even say that; - 'Modi hain toh mumkin hain".

People's Prime Minister, called by countryman or Pradhan sevak as Mr. Modi calls himself has developed trust among the common men and women of our country.

As he himself is Atmanirbhar at this age of 73 when other people of his age enjoy their retirement, but Modiji has re-tyred his passion and vision of Atmanirbhar Bharat.

It is vital to note that, **Shri. Narendra Modi** is blessing to our country and its people. I strongly argue that, our Nation has never seen a dynamic, kind, generous and grounded Prime Minister like him. He is a mixture of Gandhiji and Shivaji and also a fine combination of thoughts of divine persons i.e. Swami Vivekananda ji and Guru Gobind Singh ji – (This is my Mann Ki Baat).

**Disclaimer and Due Diligence:**

Caution, dear readers, you may think that, the author might be a 'Modi Bhakt'. No, I am not! but I am definitely a truth seeker and a global thinker who has the ability to say whatever is right, for that matter, even if it's against myself or Modiji or any other leader of the country, in case something wrong is done. Because, I am Desh Bhakt, who wants to see our India accelerating towards growth, progress and prosperity, and its my duty to tell the truth, that Mr. Modi or for instance, Brand Modi, himself is our countries primary growth engine, who have not only promised us various things, but have fulfilled or rather delivered the dreams of many Indians into reality. Year 2014 has been the biggest game changer in India's history.

There has been a famous catering near my home, since my childhood days. I have been visiting that place and the reason to quote about it is not only cravings but also carvings - A proverb have been carved on its wall's which says - "**If satisfied, tell others and if not, tell us**". Whenever I don't like any policy or decision of the government, Supreme Court or any other body, I directly tell them via email, open letters or fax etc and not to the people. On the contrary, if I like any action, implementation or persona of any person which I strongly feel satisfied after doing my own due diligences. I assure its my duty to tell it others.

Chapter – 3

# When Were the Seeds of Atmanirbhar Bharat Sowed Internationally?

**"I want each one of my children to be a hundred times greater than I could ever be. Every one of you must be a giant - must, that is my word. Obedience, readiness and love for the cause[ Atmanirbhar Bharat] - If you have these three, nothing can hold you back [From becoming 'Viksit Bharat'].**

**-Swami Vivekananda**

## Introduction:

Today we celebrate 'National Youth Day' on 12 January in the remembrance of Swami Vivekanand born on 12 January, 1863 as Narendra Datta. In 2024, Modiji addressed youths in Nasik with zeal and enthusiasm on the occasion of Youth Day.

He was a prominent figure who introduced Vedanta and yoga to the Western world. He had extensively travelled Indian subcontinent acquiring first-hand knowledge of the living conditions of Indian people in the challenging times of India.

Touched by the sufferings of the people, he had decided to travel internationally. He started his journey to the foreign countries on 31st May, 1893.

**International Imprints:**

It was on 11th September, 1893 at the Art Institute of Chicago, he sowed the seeds of free India (Atmanirbhar Bharat) by representing our country.

Instead of starting his speech by saying 'Ladies and Gentlemen', he began with "Sisters and Brothers of America", these words or phrase were novel to the Americans and therefore, Swami Vivekananda received two minutes standing ovation from the delegates including speakers who had gathered in huge numbers(seven thousand approximately), where he talked about the Indian values of tolerance and universal acceptance.

**Nationalism & Swamiji:**

It is vital to note that nationalism was a prominent theme in Swamiji's thought. He believed that a country's future depends on its people, and therefore his teaching always used to be aimed at human development by making them Atmanirbhar and Viksit.

During his speech, even though he said 'I am proud to belong to a nation(Bharat) which has sheltered the persecuted and refugees of all religions and all nations on the Earth', he was talking about the "Universal Acceptance".

When he said;

Sectarianism, bigotry, and its horrible descendant, fanaticism have long possessed this beautiful Earth. They have filled the Earth with violence, drenched it often and often with human blood, destroyed civilization and sent nations to despair. Had it not been for these horrible demands, human society would be far more advanced than it is now. But their time has come; and I fervently hope that, the bell that was tolled this morning in honour of this connection may be death-knell of all fanaticism, of all persecution with sword or pen, and of all the uncharitable feeling between persons wending their way to the same goal. He was talking about 'Tolerance'.

And further, when he said –

"I tell you it is nothing of the kind'. If it is happiness to enjoy the consciousness of this small body, it must be greater happiness to enjoy the conscience of two bodies, the measure of happiness increasing with the consciousness of an increasing number of bodies, the aim, the ultimate of happiness being reached when it becomes a universal consciousness. Therefore, to gain this infinite universal individuality, this miserable little prison individuality must go. Then alone can death cease when I am one with happiness itself; the alone all errors cease when I am one with knowledge itself; and this is a delusion that really my body is one little continuously changing body in an unbroken ocean of matter; and Advaita (Unity) is the necessary conclusion with my other counterpart, Soul - Swamiji was trying to give us a message of happiness, oneness and self + social consciousness, which will make this materialistic world more realistic.

Most importantly, when he emphasized on the principle of 'Vasudhaiva Kutumbakam'.

If there is ever to be universal religion, it must be one which will have no location in place or time; which will be infinite like the God it will preach, and where the sun will shine upon the followers of Krishna and of Christ, on saints and sinners alike; which will not be Brahminic or Buddhistic, Christian or Mohammedan, but the sum total of all these, and still have infinite space for development; which in its Catholicity will embrace in its infinite arms, and find a place for, every human being, from the lowest grovelling savage not far removed from the brute, to the highest man towering by the virtues of his head and heart almost at one humanity, making society stand in awe of him and doubt his human nature. It will be a religion that has no place for persecution or intolerance in its polity, which will recognize divinity in every man and woman and whose whole scope, whose whole force, will be created in aiding humanity to its own true, divine nature - Vivekananda tried to show us three sides of the coin-globe i.e. humanity, divinity and unity.

**Dividing in the name of Religion results into destruction and disaster:**

Last but never the least, when the Great Soul in the form of a human, Swami Vivekananda cautioned us about the separation between the Buddhists and Brahmins, Hindus and Christians, Sikhs and Muslims, will be the cause of the downfall of India. This is why India is populated with millions of beggars, and that is why India has been the slave of conquerors for the last thousand years. He did not want a Christian to become a Hindu or a Buddhist, nor a Hindu or Buddhist to become a Christian. But each must assimilate the spirit of the others and yet preserve his or her individuality and grow according to his or her own law of growth. He wanted us to grow like a seed, which if put in the ground, on Earth in air in water and placed anywhere around it. Does the seed become the Earth? Or air? Or water? No. It will always grow up to a plant, it develops in order to its own growth principle, assimilates the air, the Earth, and the water, converts them into plant substance, and grows into a plant.

**Conclusion**:

Similarly, if we want our nation to be Atmanirbhar, we should grow like a plant, which will eventually become a huge tree, where no one from the USA, Malaysia, Canada, China, Maldives or for that matter from Pakistan divides us in the name of religion, depriving us of real human development. He wanted "to set in motion a machinery which will bring the noblest ideas to the doorstep of even the poorest and the meanest", eventually making all fellow BHARTIYAS – Atmanirbhar in all its forms and in all possible ways. [Archives – Swami Vivekananda Life and Teaching at Belur Math]

## Chapter – 4

# How Is 'Atmanirbharta', Connected to Every BHARTIYA?

**'No nation can ever hold up its head, far less take pride of place amongst the nations of the world, if the individuals of which it is comprised think of nothing but personal gain and self-glorification'.**

**-Maulana Wahiduddin Khan**

Let's understand why it is so;

India is a union of states & territories not a federation of states like USA. You know why Dr. B. R. Ambedkar used the phrase "Union of States" rather than 'Federation of States'? because Indian federation is not the result of an Agreement among the States, like the American federation which mainly comprises of various 50 states as by-product of an agreement making it the 'United States of America'. If any state in USA wants to secede from the federation it can, on the contrary, the Indian states have no right to secede from the union of our country that is India, making it --- (Ek. Bharat Shreshta Bharat).

Bharat is built on the core Bhartiya foundations guided and guarded by 'Samvidhan',

(Constitution of India), which gives various fundamental, constitutional and human rights to all of its citizens. However, very less is spoken about the 'kartavyas' or 'karyas' or ' karmas' of Bhartiyas. Therefore, we shouldn't only speak of our constitutional rights, rights and rights. But, to literally understand it's our duty to go through Article 51(A) of BHARTIYA samvidhan wherein it directs; every Bhartiya

"To uphold and protect the sovereignty, unity and integrity of India"; and

'To strive towards excellence in all spheres of individual and collective activity so that the nation constantly rises to higher levels of endeavour and achievement".

After reading it, haven't you got the answers - how and why is Atmanirbharta connected to every Bhartiya?

With regards to this, I would like to refer to a quotation by [**Seneca the Younger**]

*"Society needs more individuals who understand their duty to act, rather than merely asserting their freedoms to act. True progress arises from a profound sense of responsibility".*

Therefore, it is the duty of every Bhartiya to make Bharat Atmanirbhar (Self-reliant) in all possible ways, because even our National

Anthem (Rashtra Gaan) uses a vital phrase two times - BHARATA BHAGYA VIDHATA.

From my own perspective and after applying logical mind decoded it as follows;

Bharat means 'Apna Desh and its people (Bhartiyas) Bhagya means Destiny (Viksit Bharat) Vidhata means creators (creating Atmanirbharta). Once complied it together, it simply means that, every Bhartiya is creator of his / her own destiny, which also extends to the destiny of country i.e. Viksit Bharat (Developed India).

**NaMo wiping the Nami's (tears) of Indians:**

When Pradhan Mantri Shri. Narendra Modi declared his vision of 'Atmanirbhar Bharat' to shape the future of Bharat which aimed for a 'self-reliant and resilient India', integrated with global economy along with the current reformation process ongoing in India.

In order to drive the change and speed-up the drive for 'Atmanirbhar Bharat', three important things were done;

Firstly, the tranches in which our country needed a firm foundation were identified -

(a) **Economy**: Contemplates not an incremental change but a quantum leap so that we can convert the current adversity into an advantage.

(b) **Infrastructure**: The backbone of India's economy lies in its robust infrastructure, which plays an important role in driving our countries overall progress and acts as a catalyst for its economic growth.

(c) **System**: Which would be driven by 21$^{st}$ Century Technology.

(d) **Democracy**: A vibrant democracy will be kept intact and also enhanced, by making rule of law and other allied things simple to understand and easy to execute even by Common Man.

(e) **Demand**: In commerce, the theory of demand and supply plays a pivotal role, therefore, it is essential to smartly utilize the strength of our demand vis-à-vis the supply chain by doing proper planning and efficient management.

Secondly, to implement the measures identified in order to make these Five Pillars stable (Economy, Infrastructure, System, Democracy and Demand) an economic package of Rs. 20 lakh crore was declared. The aim of this is to make our economy strong, which will eventually result in pulling the poor out of poverty, making the farmers, including the whole agriculture sector in Atmanirbhar, to reduce the hunger by 70%, reducing the gap between haves and have nots by way of funding through various national and state level schemes including the most prominent scheme of 'Atmanirbhar Bharat Abhiyan', which is made available to and for daily wagers to the MSME's etc.

Early measures to be adopted, with regard to health, ensure supply chain, smooth functioning, and enhance the connectivity not only in the form of air, water and roadways, but also in the form of virtual and digital Atmanirbharta by way of making communication easy. By ensuring the effective and efficient measures undertaken by the regulators i.e. RBI, SEBI, IRDA etc. making strategies and policies of pro-business environment.

Last but not the least,

**'Inclusivity'** – through "Jan Bhagidari" (People's Participation).

By making the policies and implementing them through the public private partnership model. All the policies which have been drafted in the last three years are 'people-centred'. As Mr. Modi once said, "I do not want VIP culture while giving up the 'Red Beckons On the cars of (very important persons)", instead he suggested E.P.I. Every Person is Important – that every person is none other than every citizen of our nation.

Recently, various leaders have been talking about the Atmanirbharta of Self-Reliant India;

During the New Delhi Leader's Declaration (NDLD) Mr. Modi said;

G-20 Summit and 'Vasudhaiva Kutumbakam', one Earth, one family, one future - which reached 1.4 billion citizens, including all the states and Union Territories as partners: And on substantive elements, India ensured that, international attention was directed to broader development aims, aligning with UN-SDG's and the G-20 Mandate.

(A) I am delighted that, during our G-20 Presidency, India achieved the extra-ordinary by making our country not only Atmanirbhar in many ways but also taking concrete steps towards becoming a global power and peacemaker. Shri. Narendra Modi.

(B) In Gujarat Home Minister - Amit Shah;

"Prime Minister Modi wants to make 140 crore people including all the poor people 'Atmanirbhar' (Self-Reliant). Modiji has worked for improving the standard of living of 60 crore people by launching and implementing various 'Yojanas' for them.

(C) Defence Minister - Rajnath Singh

During the launch of INS Imphal said; 75% indigenous content enhanced stealth features, state-of-art, equipment and weapons domestically produced are a symbol of 'Atmanirbharta'.

(D) Finance Minister - Nirmala Sitharaman

Go local, trust local, go for a self-sufficient and self-reliant India (of course which does not mean cutting off from the rest of the World).

(E) External Affairs Minister - Shri. S. Jaishankar;

"Being Atmanirbhar important for a Big Nation like India".

(F) Union Minister - Nitin Gadkari

"Atmanirbhar Bharat not possible if socio-economic desperation does not end".

Leadership thoughts were already discussed in previous chapters however, this were discussed in different context.

Poor in country have begun to live and lead a Self-Reliant life as a result of schemes. Most importantly, Late. President Dr. A.P.J. Abdul Kalam's mission 2020, aimed at making our nation Self-Reliant his dreams have started accelerating.

**Conclusion**:

To conclude it shortly, Shri. Modiji and his team of (Action Force) have showed every Indian that, each and every life matters; for that matter - the life of soldiers (on border or elsewhere) are important, the life of workers stuck in an accident (i.e. Silkyara Tunnel) is important, the life of a sports persons is important, life of its students, teachers, youths, senior citizens, etc all vital. Indians stuck during Covid-19 or during wars and conflicts are bought back to India safely bringing the feeling of safety, security and oneness among its citizens by showing them that government and its representatives really care for the people.

There are thousands of initiatives launched by many platforms. But, most importantly our Pradhan Sevak is trying to connect with every citizen in every corner of our country through his Famous Programme 'Maan-Ki-Baat', Chai Pe Charcha, Pariksha Pe Charcha, Viksit Bharat Ambassadors, through various other platforms of MyGov & NaMo App. together. (Bridging the Gap of Ashrit-ta to Atmanirbharta).

# Chapter – 5

# Role Models of 'Atmanirbhar Bharat'

**"It's not leadership by position that allows people to succeed; it's the capacity to influence the thoughts, the feelings, the emotions, and the actions of other human beings."**
**[T. Robbins.]**

In the world's largest democracy called Bharat, there are lakhs of role models of Atmanirbharta which are known in their respective regions, states, districts, villages etc. There might be at least crore of them who are Atmanirbhars, but not known to us.

Therefore, for better purpose of understanding we will be citing few of them who are not only Atmanirbhar, but are or were legends, icons, examples, influencers and real challengers. Let's categorize them into past ones and present ones.

**Let's seek guidance from the torch bearers of 'Atmanirbhars' (seven colours of rainbow)**

(1) **Swami Vivekananda**: (Millennium Motivator)

A lot have been discussed and talked about him and his work in chapter three, but he is not only a youth icon who died before turning 40, but a character builder and a great motivator, whose thoughts have bought a sea change in national outlook of our country.

**(2) Chatrapati Shivaji Maharaj: Swarajya Rakshak**

The creator of 'Swarajya', in simple words. It (Swarajya) means sovereignty of the people based on pure moral authority, self-rule, much more than freedom from all restrains. He was master in Geo-Politics, Geo-Economy and Geo-Strategy who taught the people to become fearless against all odds and built self-reliant state. Recently, Indian navy has adopted the Rajmudra as their insignia along with his naval tactics.

**(3) Mahatma Gandhi (Father of Nation):**

By profession Mohanchand Karamchand Gandhi was an attorney, who started practicing in South Africa. Eventually, he came to India and sowed the seeds of Swadeshi, Swaraj and Swadharma to drive out the britishers and make our people and country Atmanirbhar.

(4) **Dr. B. R. Ambedkar: Architect of Bharatiya Samvidhan**.

Babasaheb was not only a barrister, an economist, or a statesman, but also an all-rounder and most importantly he was a visionary and a promoter of equality.

As everyone knows that, he was the chairman of drafting committee of our 'Samvidhan', he played a crucial role strengthening the foundation of our Nation, by building the constitution. He once said that, "the constitution can provide only the organs of state such as legislature, the executive and the judiciary. The factors on which the working of these organs depend are the people". The message which he wanted to give was; if the people are Atmanirbhar then our Nation with the vibrant constitution have to become Atmanirbhar (Self-Reliant).

### (5) Sardar Vallabhai Patel: Iron Man of India

Being a champion of integration of our nation, the iron man (Loh Purush), pushed hardly to unite India, today's 'Akhand' or 'Ek Bharat' is the result of his acumenship in uniting all the states together post-independence.

He always dreamed that one day will lead to make us samarth, swabhimani, samridh and most importantly shreshta Bharat or vikisit Bharat. World's highest statue (182 meter or 597 feet) located near Kevadia in the state of Gujarat has been dedicated to him. He played a crucial leadership role in unifying our nation. The statue is known as 'Statue of Unity'.

(6) **Mother Teresa:** (Noble for Peace):

Born on **26th August**, 1910 in Skopje, then part of Ottomen empire, after attaining the age of adulthood had been shifted to Ireland, eventually landed in her karma bhoomi Bharat.

She was recipient of Roman Magsaysay Peace prize and also winner of Nobel Peace Prize. The work she had done with own hands and by her own presence in helping the poor, healing and helping the afflicted persons was incomparable.

Though some argue various non-sense things about her, but it is vital that, no one can get down where she had served to humans with humanity, a true care given by nature and a mother to many, (whom their own family never accepted) she was "ek sahara besahara loggo ke liye".

**(7) Dr. A.P.J. Abdul Kalam: People's President:**

Formally known as '*Missile Man of India*'. He was a scientist, a statesman, a dreamer, a doer, an education easter, an author and an allrounder.

In his book 'India 2020 or Vision 2020', he strongly advocated an action plan to develop India into a "Knowledge Superpower". And wanted to make our country not only Atmanirbhar, but also viksit (developed).

In the same book he had identified five areas where our nation has core competence for integrated action.

(1) Agriculture and Food Processing;

(2) Education and Healthcare;

(3) Information and Communication Technology;

(4) Infrastructure, Electric power, Surface transport and air, water, road connectivity throughout the country.

(5) Atmanirbharta is critical in the field of technologies.

He emphasized on integrating these five resulting into the unification and advancement, ultimately leading the way to food, economic and national security.

These were the seven role models or 7 colours of rainbow who had been promoting self-reliant and whose ideas and inspirations have been implemented to create Atmanirbhar Bharat.

**Let's learn from the living examples of Atmanirbhar. (seven karma yogis or 7 wonders):**

**(1) Shri. Narendra Modi: Pramukh Jan Sevak:**

Narendra Bhai or Kaka as he is popularly known in Gujarat, have versatile experience, exposure and enlightenment throughout his life.

Even today his life is full of challenges, but now challenges do not affect him, they only make him strong. He is the all-round example of Atmanirbharta. Since his childhood days he has been doing and learning various things. He is an author, ambassador of change, politician, a sanyasi, a caretaker of Bhartiya Janta, international peacemaker, man of action and, last but not the least, a human with heart full of service to mankind and most prominently his country men and women.

As he was groomed and trained by the Rashtriya Swayam Sevak in sangh - RSS. Being physically fit and disciplined is taught to the children and youths through their shakas. They are also taught defensive sport's such as lathi-kathi etc. RSS plays a crucial role in local, regional and national disaster management activities etc.

RSS is also connected to its politically affiliated body - 'Bhartiya Janta Paksha'.

Mr. Modi used to jointly handle the day-to-day affairs of RSS-BJP joint committee since his adulthood days.

It is pertinent to note that;

Narendra Modi became the Chief Minister of Gujarat directly because before that he was General Secretary of BJP. No one thought that one day Narendra Bhai, would become chief minister that days. He not only successfully was elected Chief Minister of Gujarat for three consecutive terms, but has derived advancement in the state against all adversities. Before 2014, he was the person who had never been elected or had any direct experience of parliamentary affairs or was a Member of Parliament. In 2014 election, his popularity not only grew, but his charisma, character, challenges made him Prime Minister of India as soon as he became a Member of Parliament. (MP + PM at the same time in 2014)

When he was interviewed before he became the Prime Minister of our nation, TV Anchor had asked him - 'Kya tum pradhan mantri banneka sapne dekhte hon? He replied "Main kuch banneka nahi, kuch karne ka sapna dekhta hoon." Which simply means, that, he wanted to serve the nation after becoming the PM, instead of holding a position alone, he wanted to put the position into action to benefit the common man.

He wanted to change the system, he dreamed for new India - 'Naya Bharat', Atmanirbhar and Viksit Bharat.

The way he interacts with people irrespective of cast, creed, colour or for that matter rich or poor, he makes everyone comfortable, very humble and down to Earth Prime Minister - Pradhan Sevak.

Whether its tough decision making or his exercises and meditation routine, he lives in present. He is allrounder - from playing Garba, dandiya to dhol, from flying in Tejas - to flying kites, to do snorkelling in Lakshadweep (in order to increase the tourism in our own land), scuba diving in Mathura or even participating in man v/s wild - he does it all himself, he is a hard worker, has efficient time managements skills.

From celebrating diwali with armed forces to attending DGP and IGP seminars, from addressing students on Pariksha Pe Charcha, to getting in touch with common man via 'Mann Ki Baat' he is full of energy and endurance. Moreover, he travels throughout India and also internationally, he is multi-talented, multi-tasker and multi-trained person - which our country as a Prime Minister, had never got in past or will never get in future.

Its upto all Bhartiyas to utilize all our energies to support him and his mission of Atmanirbhar Viksit Bharat.

### (2) Ratan Tata: (Icon of Simplicity)

As we know when we think of the word 'TATA', first thing comes in our mind is trust. Mr. Ratan Tata, is an industrialist, philanthropist and most importantly a nationalist. He has been a recipient of "Padma Bhushan, Padma Vibhushan, Maharashtra Bhushan and Assam Baibhav (National). And order of Australia, Honorary Knight General Crown of Order of the British Empire (International) etc.

He was born in Surat and brought up in Mumbai. Whenever our country has faced any problem with regard to disaster, pandemic, emergency it's Ratanji, who gives first financial aid or help to our country, which is known by every Indian. He lives a very simple and decent life, always eager to help, a dreamer, and a creator of wealth, jobs, opportunities to fellow countrymen. Mr. Tata is not only a well-respected figure, but also an Idol of Atmanirbhar Viksit Bharat. He himself is an allrounder, who has a dream for Bharat - to make all round development of our nation and make our motherland once again Sone Ki Chidiya [Land of Opportunities]. There's a lot to learn from him, but what I am majorly fond of, is his simplicity (simple living and high thinking) that well suits him.

(3) **Ajit Kumar Doval: Dharmo Rakshati Rakshita** (The one who protects the dharma; dharma protects him)

National security or rashtriya suraksha is vital for every country.

Mr. Doval comes from a patriotic family, his father was in defence. He had completed his early education from Military School (Ajmer). When students learn in Military school, they are taught everything from discipline to dance, from eating etiquettes to defence skills, making them almost good in everything.

As his schooling has shaped his character in his childhood days itself, after completing his Master Degree in economics from Agra University, he joined the Indian Police Service from Kerala Cadre. His career saw upscaling.

He has been Intelligence Bureau Chief. He was also the founder and chairman of Multi Agency Centre and Joint Task Force on Intelligence before taking the charge of National Security Advisor.

He is a multi-talented and all rounder Ambassador of Surakshit Atmanirbhar Bharat. He has been a recipient of many national (including Kirti Chakra) and international awards and recognitions. But according to me he deserves more. He shall get Padma Vibhushan for exemplary services he did to our motherland, which definitely is missing from his accolades and honours.

He is a mastermind of many great things unknown to Indians. His experience insights and intuitions have enriched our nation and most importantly, safety and security have been enhanced to global levels and standards.

### (4) S. P. Somanath: ISRO Chief.

Sreedhara Panicker Somanath is an aerospace engineer and scientist serving as the 10th chairman of the Indian Space Research Organisation (ISRO).

Space is one of the most important sectors, which will dominate in coming years and generations. Whether it is NASA (USA), or other space agency public or private wants to rule the space or have their upper hand when it comes to space technologies.

Recently, on 23/08/2023, the Chandrayaan-3 mission which was not only successful, but spearheaded the soft landing on the south pole of the lunar surface where no other space agencies have reached, under the leadership and guidance of Shri. S. Somanath and his team, two vital missions became successful, one that on Moon (Chandrayaan-3) and another, space craft sent to Study near the Sun (Aditya L-1).

There are many who have contributed to our Space Centre i.e. Vikram Sarabhai, Satish Dhawan, APJ Abdul Kalam, Sathish Reddy, Tessi Thomas etc. Like them, the role of S. Somanath has been created a new record and history which no citizen of this country will ever forget.

ISRO Chief and ISRO has not only made us proud, but have made Bharat's Space Agency

Atmanirbhar by setting an example at global level. The cost in which both space crafts have been made is the biggest inventory of low cost,high performance models. His leadership will continue to guide the present and upcoming space and also scientist and researchers to aspire for space researchers' activities.

Bharat have become Atmanirbhar and the journey has now been started to make it viksit in this prominent sector called "Space".

The ancient text already gave us the knowledge together with the importance of space & planets, but now we have really started combining the old tradition knowledge with new technologies - which has resulted into massive success.

(5) **Sadhguru** - born as Jagadhish Vasudev, also known by the name of Vasudev Jaggi - is the founder and head of the ISHA foundation, based in Coimbatore, India but its network spread across the globe.

Sadhguru is not only a spiritual master, but he is a preacher, teacher and an allrounder. His Inner Engineering book and course itself has transformed the life of many in India, even across globe.

Adiyogi - Shiva, one of the most important and first yogi of this universe have been researched and studied by the ISHA foundation in order to provide best of his knowledge and practices to fellow humans making our lives more and more purpose oriented and meaningful.

In spirituality, Sadhguru is a respected and most admired figure. His knowledge and way of speaking and presenting not only seeking the attention of youngsters in our country, but even every Bharatiya irrespective of their cast, creed or status likes him and his simple ways of teaching.

Sadhguru, not only preaches spiritual knowledge, but also protects the environment by advocating various initiatives and projects such as; preventing pollution by operation, Green Hands, Rally for Rivers, Cauvery calling and the journey to save soil. He has received various rewards and recognitions globally and nationally but most vital among them is Padma Vibhushan, for his contributions in the field of spirituality, climate change activities and humanitarian Services.

Even though, there are few critics who criticize his foundation or ways of teaching yoga etc., but it is important to let go the ignorant, as for that matter, in older days even superhuman and God were criticized by ignorant common people.

However, we do not want to justify, who is right and who is wrong, but what are we trying to figure out is – whether he or his ISHA

Foundation has been vital in making our Bharat and its fellow countrymen Atmanirbhars? Of course, the answer shall be in affirmation.

**(6) M. S. Dhoni – 'Captain Cool'**

Mahindra Singh Dhoni who was born in Ranchi, in a Rajput family. He comes from a humble background.

He had started his career as a Travelling Ticket Examiner (TTE), but his hard work and dedication conquered the obstacles and successfully open the doors of cricket by providing him sea of opportunities.

He is the true or all-round Ambassador of Atmanirbhar Bharat in sports category.

From a wicket-keeper to a team-keeper or captain cool or guardian to his teammates Dhoni have played a crucial role in the world of cricket (Sports).

It is vital to note that; under his captaincy our country Bharat won two World Cups, one of T-20 in 2007 and another of Cricket World Cup in 2011, followed by many other victories including the ICC Champions Trophy. No doubt, we can never forget the contributions of Shri. Kapil Dev in winning of our first World Cup in 1983, with due respect and high regards to him and his team, they have been torching bearers of Indian Cricket.

Wicket to Cricket, Mahi not only changed the image of Indian Cricket worldwide, but also taught all of us, how to be self-reliant and self-resilient even in times of adversaries. By keeping ourselves cool, we will achieve Atmanirbharta in all sports.

(7) **Soumya Swaminathan**: - A health and wellbeing National Icon and International Personality.

Mrs. Swaminathan was born to Shri. M. S. Swaminathan and Smt. Mina Swaminathan. As her father was not alone her father, but he was also the "Father of Green Revolution in India". (Who recently was conferred with the "Bharat Ratna", the highest civilian award, for his contributions in the field of yield - Agriculture) she comes from one of the noblest and educated family.

She did her M.B.B.S. from the Armed Forces Medical College in Pune, where she learnt not only lessons of medical but also about discipline, time management and most importantly, service to society.

She has various other degrees and accolades in her kitty.

It is pride for India that, she served as Deputy Director General of Programmes (DDP), at the World Health Organization. Her guidance was helpful to our Nation during the pandemic of Covid-19.

As all of us know that health is wealth, contributions of people like her are very vital.

The way a populated country with variant of diversity and so many other issues handled the pandemic, was not only applauded by the world over, but also it showed us that, by way of proper planning and implementation, we can achieve success.

Atmanirbharta in the health sector have been achieved more than 60%, but we need to work hard for receiving 40% or attaining the goal.

Chapter – 6

# Atmanirbhar Bharat Creating "New Antar Rashtriya Sanghatan" –

**"When we look at modern man, we have to face the fact that modern man suffers from a kind of poverty of the spirit, which stands in glaring contrast with a scientific and technologize abundance. 'We have learned to fly the air as birds, we have learned to swim the sea as a fish, yet we have not learned to walk the 'Earth' as brothers and sisters." - Martin Luther King Jr.**

- Vasudhaiva Kutumbakam;
- One Earth, One Family, One Future;
- Vishwa Mitra:

Basic principle in economics says, if you want your country to grow, you have to be self-sufficient, in addition to that, once the production or manufacturing etc. is surplus, increase yours trading with other nations. In simple words 'import substitution and export promotion' will accelerate the GDP and GNP of a nation.

Therefore, Atmanirbhar does not mean that, you have to be selfish, on the contrary, it does mean self-reliant and self-resilient.

Once, Bharat becomes Atmanirbhar in majority of its sectors, the first thing, we shall be doing is that of increasing our international network not only in the multilateral dimension, but also unilaterally we have to engage with the countries who wants directly do business with us.

Let's begin the exploration journey with state level activity;

**Vibrant Gujarat Global Summit** 9th (VGGS) is also called "Davos of the East".

The vibrant Gujrat has recently completed 20 successful years. From its humble beginning as an event of international business conclave to a preferred attractive investment destination, this summit which began in the year 2003 is a vibrant example that the state which had experienced to secure setbacks one in the form of Earthquake to other in form of communal riots in Godra, can transform itself into growth by 180° degree opposite through its investment and industry-friendly policies. VGGS is a best example of PPP model (Public Private Partnership Model). The state government of Gujarat is relentlessly developing invest-friendly ecosystems by way of 'Ease of Doing Business Initiatives and by providing impeccable industrial infrastructure to not only national investors, but also international investors i.e. countries, MNC's or even international organizations. In other words, we can also say that, our Prime Minister Shri. Narendra Modi and VGGS are two different parts of the same coin, because VGGS growth is directly linked to Modiji's growth and vision and Modiji's journey from Chief Minister of Gujarat to Prime Minister of Bharat was made easy because of vibrant Gujarat. "What began as an event, the VGGS has now evolved into a venerable institution, serving as a trailblazers and trendsetter. I call upon both domestic and international industrialists to identify sector where India can strengthen its position through new development opportunities. Gujarat, through the Vibrant Summit, has showcased to the world how effective decision making and a focused approach can drive transformative change. Celebrating 20 years of the Vibrant Summit's success aims to present our nation to the world as both Viksit and Atmanirbhar" -

Shri. Narendra Modiji's words.

**VGGS** is a like example of the proverb - by **R.W. Emerson** - *'Do not go where the path may lead, go instead where there is no path and leave a trail'*.

There are various other state governments in our country, who have started following the VGGS models, in order to increase the investment in their respective states which would be directly responsible for the growth of our Nation.

Let's move on to the next level i.e. National and International level engagements;

(1) **SAARC** - South Asian Association for Regional Cooperation - is a regional organization that was established in 1985 to promote cooperation among South Asia countries. Most importantly, it was formed for socio-economic development, stability, welfare forming a kind of 'Antar Rashtriya Sanghatan for collective, Atmanirbharta of the Member State'. Only reason it did not reach it's full potential is adamant behaviour of Pakistan?

(2) **BRICS**: (Brazil, Russia, India, China and South Africa)

Recently, BRICS Summit took place in South Africa. This summit was 15th summit since its formation. As the chairship was with South Africa it had and was a responsible host, where the heads of state gathered with their sherpas and delegations.

During the summit, bodies had productive discussions on boost to global economic recovery, increased partnerships with Africa and strengthen the global South. Blueprint was created and crafted which had emphasized on -

Co-operation in the field of space and collaboration in particularly education, skill, development and technology sectors. They also had plans to protect the flora and fauna. Special insights for creating a repository for traditional medicine was endorsed.

This was the same period when our Chandrayaan – 3 had successfully made its soft and swift landing on Moon, therefore, our head of the state, Shri Modiji was glad and also overwhelmed because all other country leaders have praised him and his sincere efforts of strengthening the space programmes through ISRO and allied agencies to make them one of the elite space agency in the world.

Our Prime Minister said – BRICS means;

B - Breaking barriers

R - Revitalizing economics

I - Inspiring innovation

C - Creating opportunities

S - Shaping the future of our mother Earth.

(3) **ASEAN**: Association of South-East Asian Nations.

It is prominent to note that, like the above two discussed blocks, India is not a member country of ASEAN, but due to the increased global strength of our nation and its leaders, even

ASEAN wanted to form a partnership with our country. Therefore, 20th ASEAN – India Summit paved the way to bolster the ASEAN – India Comprehensive Strategic Partnership by introducing twelve point proposal – co-operation, spanning, connectivity, digital transformation, trade and addressing global challenges together.

But prominent focus was laid on creating a multi-model economic corridor, sharing India's digital public infrastructure, establishing the ASEAN-India "Digital Future Fund," and collective inclusivity of ASEAN – India representation in various other multilateral forums.

"Summit also laid down a foundation of first Joint Maritime Military Drill in the South China sea, wherein the Indian Naval ships will take active part in INDEX – 23 and IMSC (International Management and Sports Collage, Singapore) which otherwise have only member countries of ASEAN, Bharat is a new partner on board without being a member of trade block in Singapore.

(4) **G-20**: G-20 is a group of 20 countries coming together to form a cooperation and partnership in order to make business and relations peaceful and fruitful. Last year in 2023, the presidency of G-20 was with

Bharat. Therefore, the theme also was Bharatiya - "Vasudhaiva Kutumbakam" means whole world is one family (One Earth, One Family, One Future).

As whole world today is grappling with multifaceted challenges i.e. recovery from the pandemic, looming threat of climate change, financial volatility, debt distress and downward trend, particularly in developing nations was and conflict and scams - ultimately resulting into more and more human suffering.

Therefore, India during its presidency sought to offer the world an alternative to status-quo, by changing the mindset from GDP- centric to Human-Centric progress. Our possibilist attitude reminded the world - of what unites us, rather than what divides us.

Inclusivity, ambition, action-oriented and decisiveness were promulgated in our G-20 Presidency and the New Delhi Leaders Declaration (NDLD), was unanimously adopted by all the members states.

It is vital to note that, AU - African Union was made permanent members of the G-20, which covered 55 African Nations, making this group one of the most prominent and powerful group in the world. This added the voice of the Global South to be the mouth of multilateralism.

India under its Flagship every year conducts a very popular dialogue which is called as **'Raisina Dialogue'**, its sole purpose is to create road map for foreign vis-à-vis domestic policy and also creating a level playing platform for international community in India. Even BIMSTEC and QSD or QUAD & AKUS, 2+2 or Link-16 have been vital in serving India's national interest.

Last but never the least, India has always played an active role of promoting the basic human values and also protecting the human right - leading to the human development and most importantly bringing Peace & Prosperity. Whether it is United Nations, or World Trades Organisation or IMF, WEF, WHO, World Bank or Interpol - our country has always been involved in peace making and problem solving. World's largest Democracy or Mother of democracy in spite of its domestic and international challenge have also been successfully accelerating the sustainable development, goals, by taking a cross-cutting, action-oriented approach to interconnected issues, including health, education, gender equality and environmental sustainability. Our nation Bharat have already taken a centre stage in the global affairs - if we as youngisthan deliver our maximum energy and enthusiasm in making India more and more Atmanirbhar no one at least in Asia can be parallel to India. Working in diversity is in the DNA of the Indians, which we call it as – 'Unity in Diversity. All the Bhartiyas are born adapting and mitigating. This is not only our strength, but our trade mark.

Therefore, Bharat is Vishwamitra (Friend of the World) provided the world also respect its national integrity and does not mess with its National Security. We believe in simple rule of, 'Give respect and take respect'.

# PART – II

Chapter – 1

# Who is Attorney Manish Jadhav?

---

**"Never settle for anything less than what you deserve. It's not pride, it's self-respect" –**

**Acharya Chanakya (Vishnugupta / Kautilya)**

Born with a silver spoon into a businessman family, Manish belongs to the royal clan of Marathas of Maharashtra.

**History of Jadhav's:**

**Jadhav**: is a maternal surname or family name of Matoshree – Jijja Mata – Mother of Chatrapati Shivaji Maharaja, who was the Great Maratha Warrior, strategist, king – who had been the self-made and self-crated – Ruler of Deccan. Swarajya in Bharat was established by him. Making everyone Atmanirbhar and fearless, was his ultimate teaching to Marathas and other Athra Paggad Jati & Bara-Balutedars (18-religions & 12-communities), his character was galvanized by his mother, whom he fondly called as 'Aau Saheb'. Rajmata Jijabai was the daughter of Lakhujirav and Mhalsabai Jadhav of Sindakhed Raja. (Present-day Buldhana, Maharashtra).

Jijau married Shahaji Raje Bhosle, and their second son was Shivaji, as their first son-Sambhaji died in a war at very young age. Therefore, at very early age of 14 Shivaji Maharaj was handed over the jagir of Pune to him by his father Shahaji Raje Bhosle.

As Shivaji was a teenager, it was Rashtra Mata Jijabai's responsibility to not only train and look after Shivaji, but also to manage Pune's Jagir well and guard it and its people from evil eyes and vested interests of Nizamshah, Adilshah and Mughalshahs etc.

Jijau, herself trained Shivaji in various fields i.e. education, psychology, physical fitness, war tactics, but the most important thing she did was, she used to tell him the stories of Ramayana and Mahabharata. These stories not only helped Shivaji in understanding the core values of Shri Rama and the smartness of Shree Krishna, but these were directly responsible in inculcating profound values vis-à-vis building his good character on one hand and on the other making him a great strategist whom even the Portuguese and Britishers used to envy .

There are three things which connect Manish with Matoshree Jijau; Firstly, their surname's – '**Jadhav**', Secondly, **Pune** – which was Karma bhoomi of both Jijau and Shivaji and is Karma bhoomi of Manish and Lastly, the blessing of

**Tulja Bhavani** (Mother Goddess 'Tulja Bhavani') their common deity.

**Everything is in Name:**

**Manish**: means (Buddhi) or God of Mind i.e. (Intellect), name also have various other meanings, such as 'joyful temperament', 'soul', 'pride', 'heart' or a person with deep thinking ability, wise or knowledgeable.

His name is reflected in his character, his career, his courage, his care and most prominently his certificates.

Intellect is a blessing to mankind, but it is sad that only 20% of human use their intellect?

According to **Swami Parthasarthy**;

- Plants have only body
- Animals have body + mind
- Only humans are blessed with body, mind and intellect.

And therefore, all the suffering today we see or experience is due to "Fall of Human Intellect" (as given in his famous book's "Fall of Human Intellect and Vedanta Treaties").

Manish has found his purpose to live on this planet called Earth. The sole purpose of his life is to "L & T" means learn and teach.

As he uses his intellect to make day to day choices prudently, he also tells, teach and transfer his own insight to as many as people who comes into his contact.

It is our divine duty to share our knowledge and our experience with larger number of people, and not keeping that with only our own selves. Because, knowledge alone can transform our society into – 'Sanatan Dharma'. In today's era, if we hear or listen this word "Sanatan Dharma", we immediately either run into connecting it with a particular religion or ancient or orthodox forms of living. But in deeper sense, sanatan means eternal and dharma means doing the righteous thing. Therefore, when we club these two words together i.e. 'Sanatan Dharma', it denotes; doing righteous things, with unshakable faith, laws or beliefs of nature. For example, SUN or MOON do not shine or reflect on humans alone? Are they partial in their choices? That we will only shine on a particular – species or particular religious groups, or only on the people who worship them?

Irrespective of all such things, they keep on performing their daily duties without any classification. So, it is our duty as humans who alone have been blessed with intellect, to perform our duties like sun and moon, this becomes our Sanatan Dharma.

Recently, we have been talking about the sustainable development goals, global goals or millennium development goals, but if we inculcate the values of Sanatan Dharma i.e. the principles of Vasudhaiva Kutumbakam (the world is our family), ahimsa (non-violence) and avoid greed, jealousy, lust and anger - We will need very minimum of these goals to be fulfilled. There is a famous quote 'Ignorance is Bliss' - but it's not whole right, because ignorance towards the rule of nature may be a curse to people, planets and the overall prosperity of nature within the nature.

Time has come to realize that, everyone has Manish (intellect) within themselves, and by using your intellect, you become free from all misery, anxiety, suffering and make your life blissful, joyful, purposeful and meaningful.

**Meaning of Attorney Explained;**

**Attorney**: This word has different meanings in different jurisdictions around the World. But it simply means - a person, typically a lawyer, appointed to act for another in business or legal matters (Oxford dictionary).

Lawyers in USA are called as attorneys, in UK they are called as solicitors and barristers in India; they are called as advocates or vakils and those who practice in High Courts and Supreme Court are also called as Attorney's.

The Power-of-Attorney holder is also an Attorney acting on behalf of someone who have conferred certain powers thereupon.

The international lawyers who particularly deal with Intellectual Property Rights i.e., patents, trademarks, copyright domain names etc. are also usually called or addressed as Patent Attorney's or only Attorney.

Some attorneys are also arbitrators working with various national and international arbitration centre's as counsels or attorneys or negotiators or mediators or conciliators, based on (UNCITRAL) Model Law - particularly on International Commercial Arbitration, which applies to the different jurisdictions of the globe. It was adopted in 1985, and continues to be in operation. India is party to it.

Whether it is International Court of Justice (UN - Court) or the International Commission of Jurists (ICJ) you will find attorneys everywhere across the Globe.

Attorneys have played an important role throughout history of the world, take the examples of Attorney M. K. Gandhi (Mahatma Gandhi) or Attorney Nelson Mendela (Maddiba) or Dr. B. R. Ambedkar (Babasaheb) or Attorney Barak Obama or Attorney Abraham Lincoln, Attorney Thomas Jefferson or Attorney Franklin D. Roosevelt. Most Indian Freedom Fighters were Attorneys / Advocates / Advisors i.e. Rajagopalachari / Lala Lajpat Rai, Madan Mohan Malviya, C. R. Das, Motilal Nehru,

Sardar Vallabhai Patel, including the father of Swami Vivekananda was an Indian Attorney.

Being accustomed to the laws of land, Attorneys are not only Officers of the Courts, but are vital organs responsible in promoting the fundamental freedoms and protecting the human rights enshrined in either constitution or for that matter even in common law systems worldwide.

In order to conclude, the question raised by the chapter, until now the readers might have got the answer about - who is Attorney Manish Jadhav?

If not, let me tell you that, Manish is an Indian/International Attorney also a Patent Attorney, an Arbitration Attorney working in multiple jurisdiction and variety of fields of law, who have travelled various countries for learning and teaching Law and even appeared as an Attorney/Counsel/Amicus in different countries.

His basic qualification is B.S.L., LL.B. He has done his Master of Law in Human Rights from United Kingdom. He also holds two more master's degree in Business Administration and ten diplomas in the field of Law and Legal Research, respectively.

Since last 15 years, he has been a Legal Advisor who has delivered successful results to at least a thousand clients.

Moreover, under the Free Legal Aid - a Joint effort of Law Magnets (Law Firm) and United For Human Rights (NGO), thousands of people, mostly in rural areas, have benefitted from its awareness campaigns, legal lectures, free legal aid camps and under its flagship programme of Human Rights Week, which typically takes place in the month of December every year. Larger public events are held to educate people about their rights and duties respectively.

He has received many awards and recognitions in the field of Human Rights, Environmental Law and Cyber Laws and most of them are for Social Service and Public Policy efforts.

He is enrolled as an Arbitrator with various national and international seats / courts / tribunals and Centre's of Arbitration. He is the Chief Promoter of Green Arbitrations and a signatory of the mediation before Arbitration or Litigation Pledge promulgated by the World Intellectual Property Organization.

Lastly, whether it is the UN Court or UN Conference, he has appeared before and addressed various national, local and international issues in order to upheld the Rule of Law.

He strictly, follows the poem or oath written by **St. Thomas More,** which says;

*"I pray, for the glory of God and in the pursuit of His justice, that I, may be trustworthy with confidences, keen in study, accurate in analysis, correct in conclusion, able in argument, loyal to clients, honest with all, courteous to adversaries, ever attentive to conscience.*

*Sit with me at my desk and listen with me to my client's tales. Read with me in my library and stand always beside me so that today I shall not, to win a point, lose my soul".*

**To Conclude in short;**

Even though, it's known as 'Lawyer's Prayer' it applies to all other professionals too. Only they have to replace certain words or phrases. But what is more important is "not to lose our souls".

## Chapter – 2

# Why Manish Is Called As 'Certificate Man of India'?

**"An investment in knowledge pays the best interest" -**

**Benjamin Franklin.**

**Lessons from University called as life:**

Only failure can teach you the most important lessons of your life. You can succeed if you can look past the defeat, you can win. Manish is a living example of this statement.

His real education journey began when he failed in the $10^{th}$ standard. His mother scolded him and advised him by saying (Deegryanchi line lavun taakk) in their mother tongue 'Marathi', which literally means 'You must earn Degrees/ Diplomas/Designations in a queue. He was deeply touched by the words of his mother, whom he calls as – Matoshree or Aaiee. It was a lightening moment for him, self-realisation thereafter took him from 'where he was to where he is'.

After failing, the first thing he did was, start working in a hotel. He worked hard the whole day. Thereafter, he re-appeared for $10^{th}$ exams in the month of October, which he cleared with good marks. Even though he had cleared his matriculation, he did not stop working in the hotel all day.

Eventually, when he got admission in the college for FYJC (First Year Junior College), he used to attend the college early in the morning and also manage the hotel well in the remaining time. It is vital to note that, all his education, e-learning, and career enhancements have been self-funded. Journey of Juggling with relating to studying, seeking and serving still continues, but in different context.

After completing his Higher Secondary School in Accountancy or Commerce, he successfully secured admission for a 5 years Law Course which was called at that time as (BSL, LL.B).

Early morning he used to attend Law lectures, thereafter he used to work in his own hotel and in the evening, he used to go for attending Diploma Courses.

When he was studying the Cyber Law Diploma Course, the then President of India, Dr. APJ Abdul Kalam, was called as Chief Guest at his college function. Dr. Kalam interacted joyfully with all the teachers and students . He also asked various questions to the students, but most of the correct answers were given by Manish. The People's President was so impressed that, he said to him that, "one day with your urge of seeking knowledge you would become the "**Certificate Man of India**"; but he also cautioned Manish that 'You should never stop learning.'

After his mother's scolding, this was second time that, he was not only touched by the words of Dr. Kalam (who himself was known as the '**Missile Man of India**') And was so much impressed after seeing Dr. Kalam's simplicity that he decided to be a student for life.

Thereafter, learning never stopped for him and his compilation of certificates began. Manish always says that – 'The journey of seeking knowledge and earning certificates will only end with his last breath on his beautiful planet called Mother Earth.

No doubt, he has numerous Degrees and Diplomas in his kitty, but what makes him the **Certificate Man**?

He is not only rewarded or recognized as a certificate man, but he is a world record holder in acquiring / seeking more than 3000 certificates now. He is a big fond of technology and particularly digital learning technology. He has obtained 2000 certificates out of 3k, from e-learning alone.

He has roundabout 3k certificates which are issued by; (actually the number is more but, few certificates were unable to download)

- **Inter-Governmental or Global Organisations:** UNO, WTO, WHO, WIPO, INTERPOL, ICANN, IMF, EU, AU, World Bank, WEF, ICC, ICJ, IBA, IGF, NATO, BRICS, SAARC, MENA, GCC, NASA, IAEA, G20, ASEAN, WMO, SIAC, G7 etc.
- **International Universities:** Sr. Geoge's University, Harvard University, Oxford University, John Hopkins University, MIT University, University of California, University of Texas at Austin, Cambridge and Yale University, University of Gorgia, MBRU University in UAE, University of Peace, Leicester University (UK), Symbiosis University (Pune), SPPO University, University in West Indies and many more.

**Certificates issued by Indian Bodies**:

NITI Aayog, UGC, NHRC, CVC, ED, NIA, NCRDC, NDRF, NCB, NSE, BSE, NAAC, SCI, NCDE, IIIM, NASSCOM, FICCI, DSCI, IPR, ECI, ISRO, PMO, NCERT, AIIMS, ICMR, NDA, QCI, Parliament of Bharat etc.

**Certificates from various Ministries includes;**

Ministry of Defence, Home Ministry, Ministry of External Affairs, Ministry of Corporate Affairs, Ministry of Cultural Affairs, Ministry of MSME, Ministry of Parliamentary Affairs, Ministry of Law and Justice, Ministry of Social Justice, Ministry of Transport, Ministry of Education, Ministry of Aayush, Ministry of IT and Communication, Ministry of Tribal Welfare, Ministry of Aviation, Ministry of Environment - also include various other State Ministries.

**Sports Certifications includes;**

Marathon, Golf, Billiards, Badminton, Athletics, Valley Ball, Tennis, Table Tennis, Judo, Karate, Boxing, Cycling, Swimming, Shooting, Wrestling, Defensive and Adventure Sports and most important among them is Chess Certificate.

**Certificates in Spirituality:**

Iyengar Yoga, Daa ji (Heartfulness), Patanjali, ISHA Foundation, OSHO Meditation, Manipudma Human Development, Joy of Happiness - Dalai Lama Centre (Canada), Quantum Physics and Spiritual Growth from SSPL Foundation, Pragyan Yog Shiksha University, Vivekananda Pranayama, Dhyana, Vichara, Subbudhi Kendra, Hrishikesh Yog Samity, Haridwar Yog Abhyas Prashikshan, Ram Krishna Param Hansa Mission, Jesus Christ Learning Bible Society, the Bhagwat Geeta

Society of Enlightenment, and last but not least, 'Towards understanding Islam' Certificate Course etc.

**World Records Certificate issued by:**

Gunnies World Records, International Wonder Book of Records, Web World Records, Excellence Book of Records, Cosmos Book of Records, Exclusive Book of Records, Bharat Record Book, Gunnies Records, International Records, World Records Union, Natural Record Creator, Rashtriya Shiksha Samman Record, World Records Book, Achievers Records etc.

**Certificates from various countries:**

Bharat, USA, UK, Australia, Canada, Sweden, Singapore, Hong Kong, UAE, Mauritius, Seychelles, Kenya, Nigeria, Germany, France, Russia, Saudi Arabia, West Indies, Ireland etc.

Certificates issued to Manish for his social and human and environmental related work includes:

UNEP, OHCHR, UNDP, Sahara Memorial Trust, Vivekananda Foundation, Mother Teresa Foundation Trust, Bhimrao Ambedkar Samiti, Patanjali Trust, Swarajya - Jijamata Pratishthan and almost hundred more NGOs and NPOs have given him due recognition for his knowledge, social, human rights and environmental protection work.

Whenever I asked him about his achievement as a Certificate Man? He answers; not mere accumulation of certificates will make you a Certificate Man or Woman, but continuous learning, always seeking knowledge, wisdom and inculcating noble values into your characters will make you humble, helping and harmonious person in society, eventually making you people's Certificate Man or Certified by the majority of people as a good, intellectual and healing human.

**His famous Tag line is;**

"*Sikhna Baand toh Samajna Band, Aur Jeena Baand toh Jeetna Baand*" - If learning is stopped, understanding is stopped and if living in moment is stopped, winning is stopped."

Day-by-Day, hundreds and thousands of followers have started following his digital learning techniques and also learning through various e-learning platforms. He is definitely a trendsetter, who has given mostly the youngsters to learn, e-learn, re-learn and most importantly un-learn.

Many people today have started acquiring certificates in various fields, by getting inspired by his story and his achievements, ultimately the goal of education or learning is not certificates, but values which will help to build individual, community and society. It is always better learning something digitally instead of online games or time waste on internet of thugs etc.

Chapter – 3

# When was he called – 'Ambassador of Atmanirbhar Bharat'?

**"The country will not be a good place for any of us to live in unless we make it a good place for all of us to live in." Theodore Roosevelt.**

**Rajdoot- Jantadoot & Much More;**

The word 'ambassador' derived from the French word,"ambassadeur", which comes from the medieval Latin word 'ambactiator', ambactus, which means "Vassal". Even though, the word ambassador is synonymously used or mostly used as a prefix / title to an accredited diplomat sent by a state as its permanent representative in a foreign country i.e. ambassador / envoy / commissioner etc. But its meaning is not only restricted to this form of person.

["Vassal" – a holder of land by feudal tenure on conditions of homage and allegiance.]

For instance, a representative or promoter of a specified activity is also called as Ambassador. Similarly, campaigners, exponents, advocates, champions, supporter of cause, bakers, upholders, agents, protagonists, activity, awareness or social booster people are also addressed as ambassadors.

Sometimes, we also come across the term, Goodwill ambassadors, which are known or famous persons appointed by national or international agencies such as; United Nations, World Bank, World Economic Forums etc., to promote an organization or cause of awareness campaign.

We also usually hear that, someone somewhere is appointed as a 'Brand Ambassador' of a Multi-National Company (MNC) or a promoter of a product or any other service to add value to their product, brand or services. Even some governments at state level or national level appoint brand ambassadors to promote or create awareness among the masses about any scheme, abhiyan or initiative which is beneficial to its citizens, general public or electors and voters respectively.

These were some of the meanings or contexts where word 'ambassador' to any particular person or group of persons or for that matter, an artificial person such as company, NGO, NPO, corporate can be an ambassador.

So, the question arises, what kind of ambassador is Manish? - Is he a brand ambassador of Atmanirbhar Bharat? - Is he a goodwill ambassador of Atmanirbhar Bharat? - Is he appointed as an ambassador of Atmanirbhar Bharat by any state government or government of Bharat as a promoter of Atmanirbhar Bharat?

Simple answer to all these questions is – NO!

Therefore, the question which remains to be answered – that, when was he called – ambassador of Atmanirbhar Bharat? – by whom? – for what purpose?

Manish's journey of self-realization, self-reliance and self-resilience have always been a talk of town.

Various learned people, friends and well-wishers used to call him Atmanirbhar, but it was important to note that, when a popular magazine called (Insights Success) in its May 2023 edition addressed him as "**ALL ROUND AMBASSADOR OF ATMANIRBHAR BHARAT**". Since then, people started calling him 'ambassador of Atmanirbhar Bharat'. Things did not stop there, many social organizations, non-governmental organizations, not-for profit organizations across India, gave him award, accolades and all of them started addressing him – Ambassador of Atmanirbhar Bharat.

Initially, he requested them not to address him Ambassador of Atmanirbhar Bharat, but things regarding this didn't change much.

For his own surprise, one of his friends called him and said, "how are you Ambassador? Hello Atmanirbhar!"

He was shocked, because this friend had very little idea about Manish's progress or his growth perspective. When Manish asked him that - "how cum you are calling me the Ambassador of Atmanirbhar Bharat?"

He replied, the company where he was working with, was involved in designing a homemade product under the scheme of Atmanirbhar Bharat, initiative started by the union government, therefore when he searched by putting the words - 'Atmanirbhar Bharat', suddenly it showed him, the results allied with it on 'GOOGLE search engine, this is where he said, he came to know that - Ambassador of Atmanirbhar Bharat is Attorney Manish Jadhav?

All this was very much surprising for Manish. Eventually, when he came home and searched on his electronic device by using Google - asking it - Who is the Ambassador of Atmanirbhar Bharat? To his own sudden surprise, the Google results and its search engine showed that - Ambassador of Atmanirbhar Bharat is - Attorney Manish Jadhav. - Goose Bumps!

In a country like Bharat, the highest populated country in the world, showing his name as Ambassador of Atmanirbhar Bharat, gave him shivers. This was not only a shock for him, but also a quest to be understood? Later on, he came to know that, the search engine optimization and also artificial intelligence are responsible for showing this kind of results on Google.

However, things went more deeper into his heart, as he himself has been involved in social service, helping the needy and poor since his childhood days. Suddenly, he started feeling the urge to create awareness about various government schemes which were declared during critical period of pandemic, particularly under the Atmanirbhar Bharat Abhiyan 2020. He decided to dedicate more and more time for creating the awareness about the schemes and also started delivering free lectures on the concept of Atmanirbhar Bharat.

Because, he is very well aware that, though the 'Atmanirbhar Bharat Abhiyan', is a great initiative started by the Modi government, it wasn't just one way. It is also the duty of every citizen of our nation to make our Bharat Atmanirbhar (self-reliant), by fulfilling our duties such as, paying taxes regularly, giving away subsidies if not needed, using our surplus time for the service of our nation and its people, putting our efforts into having more and more patents, giving preferences to Indian made goods, being vocal for local, creating less wastage, using our natural resources carefully, most vitally - water, by keeping our physical and mental health proper, by electing the people representation or the government, which works for people and is focused on improving the quality of people (voters) etc.

**To conclude**, let me tell you that, Manish himself is Atmanirbhar and leads a disciplined life. He is very much patriotic, he has not only denied the high paying jobs and job offers, which were made to him by the government in Middle East and Europe with big packages and perks, but also leads a very simple life style. Moreover, he works more than 18 hours a day, out of which 5 hours are specifically reserved for promoting the Atmanirbharta mission which he has started with just 120 people, which he believes will become a massive movement of people in making our country Self-Reliant in as many as possible ways in coming years. He is a living example of not only ample knowledge or grounded person, but even a person who preferred by his own choices to stay in Bharat, instead of running or going to other countries and making their country super or enriching the foreign land by our own knowledge / know-how, for few dollars, pounds, dinars etc., even when he has sea of opportunities in other nations, he preferred 'BHARAT'. In my view, this is one of the major reasons why he is not only loyal to his motherland, but he deserves to be - true ambassador of Atmanirbhar Bharat, and an existing example who followed in the footsteps of Swami Vivekananda, Dr.APJ Abdul Kalam, Mahatma Gandhi, M.S. Swaminathan, Shri. Narendra Modi and thousands like them, who had preferred Bharat over any other country in the world. This book is also a part of initiative to create a wholesome awareness among our brothers and sisters about Atmanirbhar Bharat and why making our country Self-Reliant is so much important.

## Chapter – 4

# How Can Thousands of Atmanirbhar Ambassadors, Transcend Bharat into Self-Reliant and Self-Resilient?

**The Nation is not the Land – it is the people. In transforming the people, we shall have a great Nation – Sadguru.**

Bharat is a Country of Youth;

Bharat is a Country of Possibilities;

Bharat is a Country of Tolerance;

Bharat is a Country of Innovation;

Bharat is a Country of Bright Minds;

Bharat is a Country of Blessed Hearts;

Bharat is a Country of Spiritual Treasures;

Bharat is a Country of Peace Promoters;

Bharat is a Country of Self-Reliant and Self-Resilient;

Bharat is a Country of Opportunities;

Bharat is a Country of Global Village;

Where people from different cast, religion, colour, mind sets, culture, temperament, language co-exists for hundreds of years because of its mool mantra – Vasudhaiva Kutumbakam (World is one family).

We also call it as 'Unity in diversity', but it is important to understand – why is it so? Most of the time we think 'Unity' is the real strength of India, however let me tell you it is not just togetherness, oneness or united Bharat which is only our strength, the real strength of our nation is hidden in our 'Diversity', for that matter, can you imagine so much diverse we are that – if we dig deeper into the cultural fabric of one state to another state, way of living of one region to another region, one language to so many other languages of our country? One will understand that, it's a magic, it's a miracle, ultimately, it's God will that despite so much of variations, differences in demographic patterns, still we are One. We do co-exist and therefore Indians can mitigate and are easily adaptable wherever they go across globe.

Once **Swami Vivekananda said**;

"Give me one hundred 'believing' young men …. I will transform India into the number one nation in the entire world ……"

Swami ji, emphasis was on the word – 'believing' which inculcate two things, one of 'being' or 'to be' and the other is 'to make' it happen.

"Anything good must sprout from within so that the external body can visualize and reflect the beauty of its own splendour. He used to call this as 'Spiritual Civilization'. Further, he used to say that, it is foolish to have great expectations when the inner-self is full of negative values, views and thoughts. He wanted these 100 men with not only strong belief, but wills of iron, nerves of steel and hearts that did not know to quake or shiver ....

He preferred the youths to develop a mind full of quests which would lead them to find the ultimate truth. He proposed youths to strive for their own enhancement / enlightenment and work for the welfare of society.

Swami Vivekanand a blessing to mankind, urged countrymen to understand that, "youth and beauty, life, wealth, name and fame will vanish. Even the greatest mountains crumbled to dust. Truth alone abides. Therefore, he said 'be true to yourselves, my Lads!

Are we true to ourselves? There is no straight answer to this question, because many of us have forgotten the purpose for which we were born into human life. Though there are some who know their purpose and are determined and dedicated to fulfilling it. So, we need to collaborate, cooperate and combine that some, who had realized the purpose of their lives. Out of which, we need to carefully handpick the Bharatiyas who are not only patriotic, but are willing to devote their talent, service, care, skill, education for our nation.

There are thousands and thousands of Atmanirbhars in Bharat, who wants to make difference, who wants to fight against corruption, who wants to work for betterment of society, who wants to keep environment clean, who wants to upheld the rule of law, who wants to see humans being developed and ultimately who wants to create Self-Reliant India.

Let's form the union of these few who are willingly ready to volunteer the noble cause of creating and crafting the future of the mother of Democracy of the World. Let's start to take action on the things which matter; where we are lacking, take the example of the Great Persons, who participated in the Paralympics and bought pride and purpose with perpetuity through their practice and the spirit of not giving up.

Even though majority of us have been blessed with all the organs, with all those logical minds, with all that required abilities, what many times we lack is the willingness, the oneness, the openness to accept as everyone is as they are!

Many research organizations and think tanks have found that, there are very few problems in the existing World, but lots of them are unnecessarily create by the humans. 70 - 80% (percent) of problems we face today are man-made, i.e. climate change, health emergency, conflicts and wars, happiness indexes falling down and down, relationships between the countries, the community, the couples, the children are getting *bore,* because we have become so much *sore,* escalating it further results into dis-agreements, differences and disputes which are *more* and more.

All these are happening due to the fall of human intellect? Let's make our intellect work first, pushing our minds to create, the necessary actions for making our Bharat Atmanirbhar and ultimately, put our bodies into action for fulfilling the dream of Atmanirbhar Bharat.

We all know that, we have already come far-far away from where we had started 75 years ago, but the question is – 'is that enough?' – the answer is definitely – No!

We need to work towards the common goal of making our nation self-reliant and self-resilient-way as possible, for only one simple answer, and that is –

The increasing power of our nation – Bharat, is making the world powers envy of us. The leadership at union level have been very much responsible for the growth and development of our country, even more vital, it is the people (Bhartiyas) who have become more active and aware about the national and international threats to its integrity and national security, and therefore, we shall unify and support the national cause in making it a reality. (Unity in diversity shall be our ultimate reality and not just a phrase.)

We cannot beat darkness with darkness, we cannot conquer hate by using hate, we cannot use on religion to suppress another religion, we cannot compete with the world by using same old formulas - we need light to remove the darkness, we need love to conquer hate, we need one religion to respect another religion, we can only compete with the world when we are one nation - Bharat.

By connecting and integrating these thousand men and women of our country, we can transform our nation from 'Sapne Dekhnewala Desh' to Sapne Sakhar Karnewala Desh' (Sankalp Siddhi).

The only thing we shall not forget is the word which Swami Vivekananda said - '**Believing**' - we should not stop believing in our dream, we shall not stop believing in our potential, we shouldn't under-estimate our own selves. On the contrary -

We shall trust the process;

We shall trust the purpose;

We shall trust the pivotal leadership;

We shall test our patience;

We shall value our ethics and morals;

We shall follow the basic principles of nature, nurture and culture.

And most importantly, we should believe in our Mother Land.

This is not mere a book, this is rather a blue print of success, which will eventually transform our nation into more and more capacity building, from individual level to national level.

We urge readers not just to read this book and keep it with yourself. In fact, we would suggest that, once your reading is completed, share this book with your peers, donate it to the libraries, schools, colleges so that, the coming generations benefit from the Atmanirbhar Bharat Abhiyan and understand the role to be played by every citizen of our country in making it self-sufficient. Moreover, we also want readers to let us know, if they have the values of Atmanirbharta amongst them? or they know someone with basic qualities mentioned in this book, please connect them to us, so that we can form the sanghatan of Atmanirbhars.

## Chapter – 5

# One Man, Many Shows: Leading the Way to Atmanirbharta – Swayam Sevak to Rashtriya Sevak.

**The nation is formed by its people and the people are formed by their character. - Chatrapati Shivaji Maharaj.**

**Cities Contribution in Building our Nation:**

**Pune** is also called Punya Nagri, means land of good deeds. Pune is also known as Oxford of East. Pune is cultural capital of Maharashtra, because people in Pune are very much attached to its traditions and ancient culture can be experienced in every corner of the city.

**What makes Pune so Unique?**

Take the example of Pataleshwar cave temple dedicated to the God Shiva was formed and built in 8$^{th}$ Century. The Shaniwar Wada, is also an integral part of Pune city and Pune's people.

As discussed in earlier chapters, Pune was Karma Bhoomi and Jagir given to Chatrapati Shivaji Maharaj. He got crucial lessons from his mother and various other gurus during his stay in Pune.

The city of Pune has been vital as it has produced lots of history makers, trend setters, freedom fighters, educationists, environmentalists, scientists, artists, economists, activists, socialists, nationalists, women activists, doctors and so on.

From Shivaji's Swarajya to Freedom Fighter Bal Gangadhar Tilak's saying (Swaraj Mazha janmasiddha Adhikar Ahe) which simply means – self-government and independence is our birth right, are promoted from Pune.

From Peshwa Bajirao to Rani Laxmibai (Maharani of Jhansi) have their roots embedded in Pune.

From Mahatma Gandhiji's stay in Aga Khan palace to the crucial role played by Dr. Babasaheb Ambedkar during Poona Pact, Pune have been prominent in freedom struggle.

Take the examples of Savitribai Phule, Fatima Sheikh, Mahatma Jotiba Phule, Pandita Rama Bai, Dhondo Keshav Karve, Acharya Vinoba Bhave, Acharya Atre, who have played crucial role in shaping the education system, from child education to women education of widow re-marriage were taken forward fearlessly by these great souls in Pune.

From great saints such as Sant-Dhyneshwar, Sant Tukaram, to spiritual and yoga masters i.e. Yogacharya B.K.S. Iyengar, Meditation Master – Acharya Rajnish (OSHO), Swami Parthasarthi a world renown Philosopher, Swami Kuvalayanand who founded Kaivalyadham to Swami Chinmayananda Saraswati of Chinmayananda Mission, Meher Baba to Baba Jaan, had made Pune their Karma Bhoomi.

Whether It is Music or Singing, Humour or Cartoonist, Scientist or Economist Pune have produced best among the best; Pandit Bhimsen Joshi to Lata Mangeshkar, Comedian Pu. La. Deshpande to Cartoonist R.K. Laxman and scientists like Dr. Raghunath Mashelkar to Economist Mr. Vijay Kelkar, the present NIA Chief. Sadanand Date belongs from Pune and all of them loves Pune. It's interesting that, the first female President of India, Smt. Pratibha Tai Patil, also resides in Pune, after postretirement.

It is pertinent to note that, India's largest command i.e. The Southern Command is located in Pune along with AFMC, and also National Defence Academy, DRDO, IISER, IITM, GIPE, SIU, MIT-WPU, BORI & Deccan Collage are integral parts of Pune. Pune has its own Think-Tank, i.e., Pune International Centre (PIC) which is a prominent policy promoter of Atmanirbhar Bharat.

Political leaders such as Bal Gangadhar Tilak, S.M. Joshi, Balasaheb Thackeray, Sharad Pawar etc. are born in Pune.

Recently, during the Covid-19 Pandemic two vital organs (organizations) played a very crucial role in controlling the pandemic, not only in India, but World over, that are from Pune. Firstly, the National Institute of Virology which was founded in 1978 and Secondly Serum Institute of India, who produced the Covid-19 vaccines, which not only showed India's resilience to the globe, but also increased it healthy diplomacy power in the world of uncertainties. At least, 200 Padma Awardees are from Pune, making it City of Boodhijivi Lok (Intellectual Creatures).

Pune district have given two most top judges of Supreme Court i.e. Shri. Y.V.Chandrachud (former Chief Justice of India) and his son the present Chief Justice of India, Shri. Dhananjay Chandrachud along with various other legal luminaries.

In Army, Navy, Airforce, many stalwarts are from Pune, i.e. Former Army Chief- Gen. M. M.Naravne, Shekatkar Sir, who headed vital shekatkar committee on Kargil War are few examples.

There is a popular saying - "**Pune Tithe Kay Une**" in Marathi, which literally means city of Pune has everything.

This city of Pune has been instrumental in producing India's top most doctors, scientists, lawyers, politicians, educationists, researchers, innovators, environmentalists, social activists, gender champions, Human Rights activists, philosophers, global thinkers, spiritual personalities, yogis and saints respectively.

**A Self-made Stalwart:**

Manish belongs from a businessmen family. Even though he had been blessed with all the best comfort since his childhood days, he never always enjoyed all the comforts.

He used to work in various business ventures which his father owned jointly with other HUF's. Mostly in summer vacation, he used to utilize the time in learning and understanding the manufacturing and productions process in the factory owned by his family. As he comes from a joint family, staying together with or without difference was naturally taught to all of his siblings and cousins.

During summer vacations, looking after father's business was fun and thereafter it was followed by playing various games, sports and other allied activities.

However, it was after his failure in matriculation, he started working in hotel and worked very hard. He used to be a manager, he used to serve food to the customers with boldness, without shying away, due to the simple reason that, he was son of most respected person in his community. Thereafter, learn and earn became an integral part of his life. The roots of all this were sowed when he was enrolled in NSS and Scouts, where the students are asked to serve the community, to serve the humanity, to serve the needy.

There was a concept called 'Khari Kamaii', particularly in scouts and guides 'Khari Kamaii', means you were sent to work as a helper, as an attendant, as a sales person or as a worker, and the wages you get there was called as 'Khari Kamaii', similarly like earn and learn schemes.

Many a times he also used to attend 'Shakhas' run by the Rastriya Swayam Sevak Sangh, in which various sports activities, discipline, time management, exercises and learning through ancient scriptures used to take place. All these little things have largely shaped his characters, career and care for society.

Even today most of his daily chores are done by himself. Wherever it is possible to serve. He is always ready and willing to serve the humanity, community and society. He says unless and until you yourselves are not Atmanirbhar, how can you say others to become Atmanirbhars?

Nature have given us all, only thing is that, we have forgotten to utilize it properly. Due to our laziness, we find out short-cuts to success. We do scams, we commit crimes, most of us wants easy money, which today have become a harsh reality, that most of the human do not want to work, forget working for others or community or society, they even don't want to work for themselves? As discussed in earlier chapters that we have lost the purpose, for which we were born as humans.

He strongly believes that, unless and until, you work on your own selves first, i.e. on your body (by keeping it in a proper shape), on your mind (by keeping amygdala in check), on your intellect (by keeping clear distinction in what is right and what is wrong), whatever you'll choose to be, will happen! choice is ours – To make ourselves prudent, progressive and pragmatic.

**An Icon of Amplifying Intelligence:**

Most people think that, the meaning of intelligence and intellect is one and the same. But it is not true. Intelligence means gathering of information, collecting data or acquiring knowledge; however Intellect means how to use that information or it simply means the ability to do righteous thing.

Therefore, I would say Manish is an example of combination of 'intelligence and intellect'. Because he has acquired many degrees, many diplomas, many more certificates which one could not even imagine? All this is in form of intelligence. But when he uses his energy to wake-up at 5 a.m., do yoga, do meditation, go for trekking etc. or he does daily chores, he performs all his personal and professional commitments, determination with utmost due diligence, discipline - or otherwise by not consuming alcohol, by not smoking cigarettes, by not going for playing gambling, betting or parting or dance or pubs, this is where he is using his intellect.

Everyday he wants to learn something new, everyday he wants to talk to a new person, everyday he wants to bring smile on the face of a stressed person, everyday he feeds cow, stray dogs, cats etc, everyday he loves to care for nature and environment, everyday he wants to help at least one person, everyday he teaches something new to the children, everyday he acts as an activist for social cause, everyday in spite of failures, shortcomings or job not done, he reminds himself '**picture abhi bakki hain mere dost**', everyday he express gratitude towards god for creating him as human, everyday he feels he is great, because God does not create GARBAGE.

**The Man of Multiple Talents:**

Manish is a good son to his parents, he is a good brother to his siblings, he is best buddy to his friends, he is a great husband to me i.e. his wife and definitely a best father to his son, a caring uncle to his nephew and nice, a trustworthy lawyer to his clients, and also service oriented person for society.

He is advocate, arbitrator, athlete, author, artist, advisor, ambassador, all rounder, academician, analyst, agriculturist, adventurist, and most importantly Atmanirbhar.

He runs an NGO called – United for Human Rights, which was founded in 2011. Since then, it has been instrumental in fighting injustice, slow bureaucracy, corruption, nepotism, human rights protection and promoting human values and duties towards self and society.

He has been associated with various national and international organizations and Global and local think tanks. Currently, he holds 'C' Level designations of few different entities, such as – A Law Firm, NGO, NPO, LLP and a Company.

He is also an expert in fields of human rights, environmental laws, climate change, national security, international relations, sustainable development goals, peace-making, cyber laws, mediation, arbitration, social justice, public policy, strategic thinking and social services respectively.

**Hobbies & Honours:**

Moreover, he has won 50 plus medals and 26 trophies and also has received national and international awards, records and recognitions.

He likes to collect, vintage watches, rare coins, rarest stones, unique arts, pens, stamps, buttons, toy guns and antiquities. He always says that, hobbies keep him happy, healthy and harmonious.

He has travelled various parts of our country and also travelled many other countries and continents to study their culture and customs.

He enjoys playing various instruments, dhol, tasha, Djambe, Drums, Mouth organ, Casio, tabla, flute, kalimba etc. and also loves listening music, performing traditional dance.

He is of the firm view that, the purpose of human life is to serve humanity vis-à-vis caring for nature and other creatures too. He also keeps saying that, "As our globe is round in shape, therefore God has made him all-rounder, in order to make all-round development of our Mother Planet - Earth.

The ultimate aim of his life henceforth, will be devoted in making Bharat Atmanirbhar. He is not just Ambassador of Atmanirbhar Bharat, but he is an ambassador of change, he is an ambassador of peace, he is an ambassador of people, he is an ambassador of planet. He has already begun his journey from being a **Swayam Sevak to Rashtriya Sevak**.

We appeal all the Atmanirbhars to join the mission of Atmanirbhar Bharat to make it a reality and achieve the goal at fullest.

Chapter – 6

# Atmaparikshan, Atmaprashikshan, Atmavishwas: A Way Forward in Transforming Atmanirbhar Bharat To Viksit Bharat.

---

**"The key to being prepared for the unknown isn't about predicting the future, but about developing an-unwavering resilience and composure to confront whatever may arise" -**

**Marcus Antonimus Aureluis.**

Let's now get deeper into understanding why independence or freedom matters? Why democracy is so much important? What are pros and cons of democracy? Why saying unity in diversity is not enough? Why economic progress alone will not create a welfare state? How long will it take us to change our colonial mindset? When will our constitution create real parity?

All of the answers to the questions raised above lies in three 'A's:

1) **Atmaparikshan**

2) **Atmaprashikshan**

3) **Atmavishwas**

1) **Atmaparikshan:** (Self-Interospection)

Everyone knows that britishers ruled India for almost 90 years, this period was also called as the British Raj, which is a combination of British means, people from Britain (English) and Raj (in Hindi) means the kingdom or empire, simply means that India was their kingdom or they were ruler of India.

Wherever they went to rule or expand their empire, they followed a policy of "Divide and Rule". In our case they created enmity between Hindus and Muslims, during their rule and even after their exit, they created two states out of one Bharat and that two states are known as India and Pakistan. The people who were directly or indirectly radicalized by British or their agents, went to Pakistan, forming a totally new country in name of religion i.e. Islam. However, it is pertinent to note that, not all Muslims went to Pakistan, the Muslims who stayed back in India were not asked to stay here forcefully, neither were they lured by the majority by offering them some reward or recognition. The Muslims who stayed back in India were not only liberal or logical, but lovers of their original Mother Land i.e. Bharat. They remained in this country by their own preferred choice. Because they trusted democracy, they had faith in the constitution, they had feeling of brotherhood with other religious people and communities with whom they co-habited, co-existed and most importantly co-operated, since Pre-independence Period.

Today, Pakistan is a failed State, which not only committed genocide against their own people (Bengali Muslims), but even today crime, terrorism, threats to religious freedoms, gender inequality, corruption, anarchy and most importantly hegemony of army have brought its economy so much down that every now and then they are bailed-out by the IMF or either get paid by foreign funders i.e. Saudi Arabia, Turkey, USA or China.

It is true that, Britishers are now-a-days replaced by the Canadians who support illegal activities of the Khalistani people to divide the people in Punjab, or elsewhere in India and the world. Is it true? That the Dragon does not want our country to be sustainable, stable and strong. Therefore, keeps on meddling in IOR region, Af-Pak region into the Iran or in Maldives and Nepal to create problems to us.

It is true that, the Westerners want to divide the Christians in our country, by converting one tribe and later on dividing them with the other tribe following Hinduism?

It is also a fact, that the politicians themselves have become Britishers, who just before the elections divide the people on the name of caste, culture, colour, community or religion? Is it a reality that, majority of the world powers do not want our country to be strong and self-sufficient?

Truth about all the statements above is mostly true, because large numbers of Indians are sleeping or rather ignorant to the root cause of the problems discussed above or either they get carried away by their own emotions, if someone instigates them, it is the duty of separatists, perpetrators and radicals to create problems by dividing us, to serve their own selfish motives, intentions and interests. Are we really so dumb that, even today after 75 years of Independence are dependent on someone who can tell us, what is right and what is wrong for the betterment of society, and particularly our own country and community? All the answers lie within us, only thing which we need to do is – self-introspection and introspection of separatists, perpetrators and pauper politicians, shall be revealed to all the fellow citizens.

Unfortunately, many youths today follow the wrong examples of westerners i.e. drinking alcohol, smoking, partying in half-naked dresses, getting addicted to porn and following anti-social media trends, only playing online gaming or scrolling, surfing, strolling. Even teenagers have fallen prey to this kind of traps – We say that, future of our country lies in the hands of youngsters, are they truly aware of the impact of their actions? On the contrary, the people with abilities are not getting right opportunities, so that they can make difference, they can create new India, they can be well equipped to face the upcoming challenges in near future? We all together have to find solutions to these problems, right answers to these kind of difficult problems - Yes! **Atmaparikshan** is the master- key to all these lacks or lacunas.

2) **Atmaprashikshan**: (Self-Defence)

Once we have identified the root cause of the evils in our society, we need to fight it with our self-Defense mechanism. We shall also find the collective areas of improvement, because the sooner we begin to strengthen ourselves and our country into these areas, sectors or fields, we will be able to achieve many of them before our targeted timeframe.

War and fear, mongers in near future, the individuals, the groups, the masses, the society, the country, which is prepared with its self-defence system will not face much repercussions during such hard times, only the nation which is busy entertaining, enjoying and erring itself from knowing the harsh realities of this globe will find it difficult to cope-up during sudden emergencies created by nature or for that matter conspired by other nations.

Moreover, in today's world, we cannot just rely on traditional warfare techniques, we have to build cyber defence system to tackle the threats of Cyber Security, Artificial Intelligence challenges of deep fakes, dark webs or even space wars in future cannot be ruled out. Therefore, the broader view and approach we have today, the most powerful defence mechanism our nation can built on its own, and keep itself future proof or uncertainty ready for any and everything.

It has also been observed that, the social faith or cultural equilibrium gets easily disturbed, even if we are provoked by the mindless creatures. No! We shall not become victims of such events, we should apply our logic, take appropriate advice from the learned and respond or act prudently. Because the external powers are aware that they cannot win war against us directly, pulling us into the conflict zones or by attacking us through missile etc. Therefore, they keep on disturbing our internal security in order to harm our national integrity & unity by conducting riots, creating differences in the name of religion, supporting particular religious groups by showing them sympathy, pressurizing our country through international pressure tactics for things not done or wrong not committed by us.

Every sector shall be well equipped with the self-defence mechanism, whether its infrastructure, its economy and energies, its ecology, its transport, its communications, its information technology, its aviation, its naval power, its military power, its systems management, its education field, its skill development, its women and child welfare or it's in the field of sustainable development goals, in every sector. We need to give our attention and eventually convert that attention into action to bring self-reliance and resilience by attaining self-sufficiency. *Atmaprashikshan* has vital role in activating the 'White Blood Cell (WBC)', and making our sytem immune in order to fight the necessary infections and diseases occurring in our country.

3) **Atmavishwas**: (Self-Confidence)

No one could be the better example than Swami Vivekananda on developing self-confidence as 'Nationalism was a prominent theme in his thought, he believed that the country's future depends on its people and his teachings focused on the human development which can only be achieved by self-confidence'. Ultimately, he wanted 'to set in motion a machinery which will bring noblest ideas to the doorstep of even the poorest and the meanest'.

Our present National Security Advisor – **Shri. Ajit Doval**, who is also the founder director of

'Vivekananda International Foundation', recently said;

*"Your decisions are not right or wrong, what happens is that, you take a decision , but you don't work towards it, so taking the right decision is less important than making the decision right. After you have taken a decision, then it's your bravery, it is your commitment, it's your foresightedness. It is your sense of tolerance, your ability to take this thing, that you make the decision right. And so, concentrate more on action then keep on changing the decisions, you have taken a decision go ahead".* This is one example,Our countries National Security Policy, instead of changing every time has very well remained same since 2014 i.e. Permanent National Interest, Integration of Masses, and inclusive growth. no compromise on National Security, making Bharat's Rashtriya Suraksha as its first and foremost priority. Likewise, when we will change our focus from individuality to society, we will get the clear picture, what needs to be done for the betterment of our society, community and country respectively.

One person, like Shri. Modi thinks of changing our country, its stature, its status, its stability and its story of success, many others get impressed and inspired by him, start working on the goal, along with him, start connecting other like-minded individuals, small groups, regional and state level groups, by ultimately forming a strong team at national Level. All of them working day and night, all of them dreaming and creating a driving force by forming a synergy of change maker's, records creators, innovators, tuff negotiators, dream catchers, aim achievers, the nation builders, unity promoters, enmity enders, peace preachers and so on. Why do you think people get attracted, attached & awaked or fascinated by him or his aura? Because of only one reason and that is AtmaVishwas!

Therefore, if anyone asks me to define Modi ji in simple one word, I would like to say 'he is atmavishwas or atmavishwas is him'. Many times, self-confidence is not only seen, but also reflected or felt into his actions and his interactions with his colleagues in parliament, with counterparts on various international platforms, while interacting with the students, labour's, victims, Paralympics, sport's personalities, actor's, activists, artist's, police, defence personals priest's, presidents, and poor people alike. Whether it is naman to nari shakti or working towards garibi mukti, and nari samman to garib kalyan, he gives his confidence to everyone who needs it. Moreover, he always keeps on saying affirmative or possibilist statements like: 'Modi Hain Toh Mumkin Hain', 'Bharat Viksit Hoga Ye Modi ki guaranty hain', 'Atmavishwas se Atmanirbhar ka safar' and now he along with crores of bhartiyas have taken sankalp to make our nation 'Atmanirbhar and Viksit by 2047', which he calls as **'Sankalp Siddhi'**, 'Amrit Kaal', 'Azadi ka Amrit Mohatsav'', he wants to bring Ram Rajya. Ram rajya does not mean to build Ram Mandirs everywhere in our country, but it does mean, rule of righteousness, happiness & peacefulness.

To support his Sankalp Siddhi, I have added a tagline to it --- "**Amrit Kaal Ke Ane Wale Saal, Atmanirbhar Aur Viksit Bharat De Naal**", this simply means that the coming golden years of Amrit Kaal shall be dedicated and committed in making Bharat both, a) Atmanirbhar and b) Viksit.

Let me tell you, that self-confidence is not only about self? It can be also about the teamwork which can achieve the dream work, it is also about the confidence of keeping ourselves united through thick and thin situations like, pandemic, conflicts, riots, natural disasters, climate change effects by burring our personal differences and also conquering selfish motives and intentions.

*Atmavishwas* is the ultimate foundation of character building, which actually have more wider meaning than self-confidence. Once your character is built upon values based on righteousness, the real process of progress with regard to people, planet and personality has begun and this process of perpetual progressive practice will result into highest form of rationality, nationality & universality. However, all this is easy to say, but difficult to act upon. Whenever, we stand in front of the mirror, what we see is the reflection of our own body and not our own self. Going more deeper, when we stand in front of the same mirror, but into absolute darkroom, can we see our reflection? not maybe! However, we can feel our own self in the same darkness. Through this illustration mentioned above, I want to make the reader's and seekers to understand the concept of Atmavishwas, because many a times you are not able to see it, but you may very well feel it.

Likewise, India's growth story in coming year's will not only be reflected and seen, but will be felt by every citizen of our country, provided we should start working on it, by practicing self-confidence and self-control, having the confidence in union leadership, by having the confidence on the abilities, by conquering the fear, by reminding ourselves that we are full of Atmavishwas of becoming Atmanirbhar by all means and standards.

**Bharat** do not intend to rule the world, but definitely wants to cultivate the idea of 'Vasudhaiva Kutumbakam', (World as one family) among its peers on this wonderful Planet.

## A way forward in transforming Atmanirbhar Bharat to Viksit Bharat by 2047:

'Self-realization is the greatest wealth' --- Epicurus.

There are hundreds of things which we need to improve in our country in order to become Viksit. Few may say, economy, education, entrepreneurship, environment, infrastructure, skilling, gender equality, digital wellbeing, technological advancement, zeroing the hunger, eradicating the poverty, slowing down of the corruption, nepotism and favouritism, may solve the problems, eventually making us Viksit by 2047?

However, three very much essential things which are less spoken about, shall be given more and more importance than any or every other thing mentioned above, which I think and strongly argue are the signs of the truly developed world or Viksit Jaag.

### 1) Democratic Accountability; First Priority

When we call our country the 'Mother of Democracy' or define it as largest democracy in the world, We many a times forget that, Democracy is for the people, of the people & most importantly by the people. We also do not see it through the lens of accountability and transparency. Democracy is not only about Elections? Then why are we making it Election

Centric ? Democracy is refined and defined by the freedom to differ and dissent, because democracy does not automatically guarantee us our freedoms and rights, even though, we may have political democracy by conducting elections after every five year's but we cannot guarantee liberal regime, which may give us freedoms of speech, expression, assembly or religion? That, individual freedoms can't be enforced without social cohesion. When we say – 'Unity in Diversity', as already discussed in previous chapters, the purpose behind using this term is to provide a holistic view, that people irrespective of their individual beliefs, faiths and interests, would acknowledge a common national identity and collective national interest.

**2) The 'Rule of Law': Ultimate Game Changer;**

When we say rule of law, what actually are we defining it with? Mostly we define it with the Bharatiya Samviddhan, particularly under the Article's 14 & 21. Art.14 says equality before the law and equal justice to all --- What does it mean? It means that, everyone should have equal access and opportunity to seek justice. It also means that the laws are applicable to everyone equally. For an example, anyone who breaks the law, no matter how powerful, positioned or influential one could be, if he or she commits the wrong or crime or infringement, will be caught and punished. And Article 21;

Protects the essential Right to Life and Personal Liberty of its people.

Moreover, general public or common man and woman also will be protected from the tyranny of the State, oppression and suppression of its own people by the government, politicians, the British bureaucratic mindset and the business persons, and avoid diminishing value of dissent. Rule of law acts as ombudsman, watchdog by keeping the power, politicians & paupers in check.

There's a famous quote by John Acton: "***Power tends to corrupt, and absolute power corrupts absolutely.***" Therefore, absence of 'Rule of Law', in any society, community or country will most probably result into anarchy, oligarchy, authoritativeness and abuse towards its own people. See the examples of Sri Lanka, Pakistan or many other countries in Europe, Arab and African world where rule of law has miserably failed, citizens are the ones Who have not only suffered but eventually treated as subjects & slaves of dictatorship of its forge leaders.

### 3) Strong Institution: Master Key

It is prominent to note that, the rule of law and democratic accountability, does not operate in vacuum, because it should be accompanied with strong Institution. Perhaps, strong institution doesn't mean an authoritarian government that rules with an iron fist towards its people. On the contrary, it does mean that, a state which deploys sovereign power to make and enforce rules or laws made keeping in mind the democratic values and principal of natural justice. Such states shall deliver public welfare i.e. safety and security, environment and education, health and happiness, the State that, promotes unity and uniformity and last but not the least, promotes innovation and all other kind of inclusion. Because, good governance and low levels of corruption are two sides of the same coin, which can create a strong institution. The institution which whole heartedly, serves it's people and deliver promises made during or before the elections by using their problem solving skills. There shall be a fine and delicate balance between giving people their freedom to decide how they want to live and what they trust or believe, Vis-à-vis integrating them to subscribe to a national identity and nationalist belief system. Therefore, a lot of adjustments are needed to be done between the institution (government at Union and State Levels) and the people by skillfully managing and deciding the Quantum about where the institution shall be accommodative and where the people must perform their fundamental duties.

**Yes**! It is possible to make our nation Atmanirbhar and Viksit by or even before 2047, provided we just do not focus only on the quantum of growth defined by various factors and measurements but, we must focus even on the overall quality and wellbeing of its people, planet, prospective of all the citizens including the tribes, minorities and also the downtrodden ones.

**To conclude**, the journey of Atmanirbhar Bharat, began after we got our independence in 1947, however, it started accelerating mostly in last couple of decades, but speed-up only after the "Atmanirbhar Bharat Abhiyan" that was initiated and declared in 2020, in order to make our country self-reliant, self-resilient and most importantly self-sufficient at least in the core sectors. Sadly, people's participation have not been so much vibrant yet, unless and until people also take active part in larger numbers, we cannot achieve the goal to the fullest.

Therefore, the purpose of this book, once again I would like to remind, is to find and create lakhs and lakhs of ambassadors of Atmanirbhar Bharat! At least a crore of Viksit Bharat Ambassadors, to reap the benefits of Amrit Kaal, to create the level playing field even for poor and underprivileged, to manifest the Sankalp Siddhi into our daily lives and activities, so that, day by day in every possible way, we can achieve more and more. Because, we should not forget that, the population of our country will be exploding in coming years and decades. We need to change our perspective and perception towards aiming high and achieving more. The ultimate goal is to "leaving no one behind", everything is possible only if we believe! only if we have faith! only if we trust in our own selves, that one day we will and our coming generations will live happily and harmoniously in Viksit Bharat.

In **Marathi** we say --- "**Baghtaa kaay Saamil Vhaa**", which means do not just look or stare or see, but join, unite, integrate. We all are Bharatiyas instead of competing with one another it's our moral duty and responsibility to complete one another in the national spirit of brotherhood and sisterhood unitedly.

Swami Vivekananda once said; "*We do nothing by ourselves but we criticize and mock those that do (deliver/perform/achieve). This is one of the reasons for the denigration of India*".

**Jai Hind!**

**Jai Viksit Bharat!**

**Jai Atmanirbhar Bharat!**

# List of Abbreviations

AAB- Ambassador Atmanirbhar Bharat

A.U. – African Union

AI – Artificial Intelligence

AFMC – Armed Forces Medical College

ASEAN- Association of South East Asian Nations

BJP – Bharatiya Janta Party

B.S.L – Bachelor's in Socio-Legal Sciences

BSE – Bombay Stock Exchange

BRICS – Brazil, Russia, India, China, South Africa.

BORI Bhandarkar Oriental Research Institute.

Covid-19 - Corona Virus 2019

CIC – Central Information Commissioner

DRDO – Defence Research and Development Organisation

DSCI – Data Security Council of India

DNA – DeoxyriboNucleic acid

DGP- Director General of Police

DDP – Deputy Director General of Programmes

Digi-locker: – Digital Locker

ECI – Election Commission of India

ED – Enforcement Directorate

EU – European Union

EAM – External Affairs Minister

EPI – Every Person is Important

Email – Electronic Mail

FICCI- Federation of Indian Chambers of Commerce and Industry.

FYJC – First Year Junior College

Geo – Geographic

GDP – Gross Domestic Product

GNP – Gross National Product

GCC – Gulf Cooperation Council

GST – Goods and Services Tax

GOD – Generator, Operator, Destroyer (Bramha-Vishnu-Mahesh)

G-20: Group of Twenty Countries

GIPE – Gokhale Institute of Politics and Economics

Google – Global Organisation of Oriented Group Language of Earth

HRC – Human Rights Council

HUF – Hindu Undivided Family

ICJ – International Court of Justice

ICANN – Internet Corporation for Assigned Names and Numbers

ICC – International Chamber of Commerce

IGF – Internet Governance Forum

IAEA – International Atomic Energy Agency

ISRO – Indian Space and Research Organisation

IMSC - International Management and Sports College

IMF – International Monetary Fund

INS – Indian Naval Ship

IRDA – Insurance Regulatory Development Authority

IITM – Indian Institute of Tropical Meteorology

ICMR - Indian Council of Medical and Research

INTERPOL – International Police

JMMD – Joint Maritime Military Drill

KP- Kyoto Protocol

LLP – Limited Liability Partnership

LLB – Bachelor's in Law

LLM- Masters of Law

L & T – Learn and Teach

MBBS – Bachelors of Medicine

MNC – Multi National Corporation

MIT – Massachusetts Institute of Technology

MDG – Millennium Development Goals

MIT-WPU - Maharashtra Institute of Technology – World Peace University

MyGov – My Government

MSME – Ministry of Small and Medium Enterprises

NASA – National Aeronautics Space Agency

NDLD – New Delhi Leader's Declaration

NEP – National Education Policy

NIV – National Institute of Virology

NITI – National Institute for Transforming India

NHRC – National Human Rights Commission

NGO – Non-Governmental Organisation

NPO – Not for Profit Organisation

NATO – North Atlantic Treaty Organisation

NSS – National Social Service

NSA – National Security Advisor

NIA – National Investigation Agency

NDRF – National Disaster Relief Fund

NCRDC – National Consumer Disputes Redressal Commission

NCB – Narcotics Control Bureau

NSE – National Stock Exchange

NAAC – National Assessment and Accreditation Council

NASSCOM – National Association of Software and Services Companies

NCERT – National Council of Educational Research and Training

NDA – National Defence Academy

NaMo - Narendra Modi

OHCHR – Office of High Commissioner on Human Rights.

PIC – Pune International Centre

PIL – Public Interest Litigation

PhD – Doctorate in Philosophy

PPP – Public Private Partnership

QCI - Quality Council of India

RD - Raisina Dialogue

RSS - Rashtriya Swayam Sevak

RBI - Reserve Bank of India

SAARC - South Asian Association for Regional Cooperation

SCI - Supreme Court of India

SEO - Search Engine Optimization

SDG - Sustainable Development Goals

SIAC - Singaporean International Arbitration Centre

SIU - Symbiosis International University

SPPU - Savitribai Phule Pune University

SEBI - Security Exchange Board of India

TTE - Train Ticket Examiner

UGC - University Grants Commission

UNITAR- United Nations Institute for Training and Research

USA - United States of America

UK - United Kingdom

UAE - United Arab Emirates

UNO - United Nations Organisation

UNEP - United Nations Environment Programme

UNDP - United Nations Development Programme

UNCITRAL - United Nations Commission on International Trade Law

VIP - Very Important Person

VGGS - Vibrant Gujarat Global Summit

WBG - World Bank Group

WFH - Work from Home

WHO - World Health Organisation

WTO - World Trade Organisation

WMO - World Meteorological Organisation

WEF - World Economic Forum

WIPO - World Intellectual Property Organisation

# Notes and References


1) United Nations e-learning platforms
2) Archives from Sabarmati Ashram and Aga Khan Place
3) APJ Abdul Kalam's Book, Mission-2020
4) Indira and her famous speeches.
5) Chatrapati Shivaji Maharaj- The Great Maratha Warrior
6) The India Way by Shri. S. Jaishankar
7) Securing India the Modi way, by Nitin Desai
8) Belur Math Archives based on real life's journey of Swami Vivekananda & SV Life and Teaching.
9) Towards Understanding Islam, by Maulana Maududi.
10) Maulana Wahiduddin Khan Article's
11) National Anthem of India
12) Notes from Atmanirbhar Bharat Abhiyan
13) Dr.B.R.Ambedkar Archives in Ambedkar Museum, Pune
14) Loh Purush : Iron Man of India

15) Mother Teresa and her Works.

16) Yoga of Education by Shri. Narendra Modi.

17) Kholi Ani Vyapti by RSS

18) Tata (Book)

19) National Security Advisor, information available on its web.

20) ISRO website

21) ISHA Foundation & Inner Engineering

22) DHONI & ICC magazine

23) WHO website

24) UN web studies and webinars

25) New Delhi Leader's Declaration

26) History of Jadhavrao & Marathas Archives, at PUNE.

27) Rashtramata Jijau, Lal Mahal.

28) Vedanta Treaties and Fall of Human Intellect, by Swami Parthasarthi.

29) Lawyer's Prayer (Poem) by St. Thomas More

30) Lawyer's Presidents of USA notes.

31) Freedom Fighters And their works, article's.

32) Insights Success Magazine, May 2023 edition

33) Sustainable Development Goals and United Nations

34) Constitution of India

35) Preamble of Indian Constitution

36) Rashtra Gaan

37) Government of India websites, I.e. PMO, MyGov, NaMo, Atmanirbhar Bharat Abhiyan & Viksit Bharat Ambassadors Programme

38) The Raj (Britishers)

39) Many weekly magazines in electronic form by MyGov.

40) Articles, Notes & Analysis in leading News Papers I.e., ToI IE, HT, TH and etc.

41) Dictionaries; Oxford, Cambridge & Collins.

42) Apps Used for seeking information; MyGov, NaMo, X, and Google Newsstand.

[**NOTE & Disclaimer**: The Author, co- Author and the publisher's do not intend to copy, imitate or plagiarize anybody's work, however, sometimes the ways which we express maybe similar to avoid confusion and conflicts, we have tried to give as much as notes and mentioned references, but if in any case the work is found similar you can contact the allied persons to resolve the issues amicably].

# Epilogue

Self-Knowledge a poem- by *Khalil Gibran (The Prophet);*

And a man said, speak to us of self-knowledge.

And he answered, saying:

Your hearts know in silence the secrets of the days and the nights.

But your ears thirst for the sound of your hearts knowledge.

You would know in words that which you have always known in thought.

You would touch with your fingers the naked body of your dreams.

And it is well you should.

The hidden well-spring of your soul must need rise and run murmuring to the sea;

And the treasure of your infinite depths would be revealed to your eyes.

But let there be no scales to weigh your unknown treasure;

And seek not the depths of your knowledge with staff or sounding line.

For self is a sea boundless and measureless.

Say not, "I have found the truth," but rather, "I have found a truth."

Say not, "I have found the path of the soul." Say rather, "I have met the soul walking upon my path."

For the soul walks upon all paths.

The soul walks not upon a line, neither does it grow like a reed.

The soul unfolds itself, like a **lotus** of countless petals.

### Crafting the Conclusion

We are countless petals of this **lotus**, our national flower, let's cherish what we have, let's be proud of our ancient culture, let's grow together in the spirit of brotherhood & sisterhood, and let's celebrate the differences, by uniting, because all the fingers of the same hand are not alike, still we do not call them five-fingers but we call it one hand? let's commit ourselves to make our Bharat – Viksit & Atmanirbhar!

1. Nevertheless, a famous sufi saint – "**Baba Bulleshah**", use to say '*Geeta padhaa, Quran padhaa, lekinn apne aapko padhaa hi Nahi*'! It simply means we read Bhagwat Geeta, we read Quran and many other holy books etc.

But we are unable to know ourselves, this is the main cause of every evil in the society. Before, getting judgemental about this book, or for that matter any other person's, I request you to begin the quest of understanding yourselves first, things & relations will become easier to handle. If unknowingly we have committed any mistakes in writing or any other sense, please feel free to reach us, we would like to hear your complaints and also would glad to receive your compliments with love, if the readers find the book interesting, please pass on this book to them who are interested in making Bharat Atmanirbhar and do not forget to join the Ambassadors of Atmanirbhar Bharat Sanghatan in order to strengthen the agenda of Viksit Bharat.